There is a transforming force emerging in America today. A new generation of black leaders is taking in hand the torch of inspiration that history now offers. How desperately we need them. Though they stand respectfully on the shoulders of those heroic African Americans who have come before, they do not feel themselves limited to the societal solutions of an earlier age. They question. They probe. They innovate. With one hand they grasp time-honored values of faith and progress, and with the other they fashion a future for their age that is without parallel in history. Bishop Harry Jackson's *The Truth in Black and White* is a trumpet call of this new leadership, and we do well to hope that many in our age both hear and answer the words of this heroic man.

—STEPHEN MANSFIELD
The Mansfield Group
Nashville, TN

I have personally known Harry Jackson for many years. I stand in awe of the wisdom he walks in with the knowledge he has on the issues in this book. He is more than qualified to address controversial black and white matters because his approach is not from a prejudiced position. The words of this book confirm the mantle of greatness that rests on Harry's life. He is a modern-day justice activist for Jesus, and his light is shining from the pulpits to the political arenas of America.

—APOSTLE KIMBERLY DANIELS
Spoken Word Ministries
Jacksonville, FL

Harry Jackson continues to bring life-giving, balancing words of wisdom to the body of Christ. This sensitive and significant book is a landmark in statemanship and spiritual leadership. Furthering its worth is Jackson's character and integrity in the life he leads.

—DR. JACK W. HAYFORD
Chancellor, The King's College and Seminary
Founding pastor, The Church On The Way

THE
TRUTH
IN BLACK
& WHITE

HARRY R. JACKSON JR.

FRONT
LINE

A STRANG COMPANY

Most STRANG COMMUNICATIONS/CHARISMA HOUSE/SILOAM/FRONTLINE/ EXCEL BOOKS/REALMS products are available at special quantity discounts for bulk purchase for sales promotions, premiums, fund-raising, and educational needs. For details, write Strang Communications/Charisma House/Siloam/ FrontLine/Excel Books/Realms, 600 Rinehart Road, Lake Mary, Florida 32746, or telephone (407) 333-0600.

THE TRUTH IN BLACK AND WHITE by Harry R. Jackson Jr.
Published by FrontLine
A Strang Company
600 Rinehart Road
Lake Mary, Florida 32746
www.frontlineissues.com

Unless otherwise noted, all Scripture quotations are from the New King James version of the Bible. Copyright © 1979, 1980, 1982, by Thomas Nelson, Inc., publishers. Used by permission.

Design Director: Bill Johnson
Cover Designers: Marvin Eans, Bill Johnson

Library of Congress Cataloging-in-Publication Data:
Jackson, Harry R.
    The truth in black and white / Harry R. Jackson. -- 1st ed.
        p. cm.
    Includes bibliographical references.
    ISBN-13: 978-1-59979-268-2
    1. African Americans--Religion. 2. Christians--Political activity. 3. Christianity--United States. 4. Christianity and politics--United States. 5. United States--Church history--21st century. I. Title.
    BR563.N4J325 2008
    277.3'08308996073--dc22
                                        2008007891

First Edition

08 09 10 11 12 — 987654321
Printed in the United States of America

Congress shall make no law respecting an establishment of religion, or prohibiting the free exercise thereof; or abridging the freedom of speech, or of the press; or the right of the people peaceably to assemble, and to petition the Government for a redress of grievances.

—First Amendment
Constitution of the United States

I look forward confidently to the day when all who work for a living will be one with no thought to their separateness as Negroes, Jews, Italians or any other distinctions. This will be the day when we bring into full realization the American dream—a dream yet unfulfilled.

—Martin Luther King Jr.
August 28, 1963

[C O N T E N T S]

A Prophetic Moment

THE ULTIMATE MEASURE OF A MAN IS NOT WHERE HE stands in moments of comfort and convenience, but where he stands at times of challenge and controversy. The true neighbor will risk his position, his prestige, and even his life for the welfare of others. In dangerous valleys and hazardous pathways, he will lift some bruised and beaten brother to a higher and more noble life."[1] When Dr. Martin Luther King Jr. wrote those stirring words in 1963, he was up to his neck in controversies, struggling to build a movement and gain support for the cause of civil rights at a time when the resistance from forces seen and unseen was overwhelming.

He had carried out successful voter-registration drives in Georgia, Alabama, and Virginia by that time, and in August of 1963 he would lead the now-legendary March on Washington. When he addressed that crowd of nearly a quarter million men, women, and children from the steps of the Lincoln Memorial, Dr. King laid out for all Americans a dream of reconciliation and renewal that would change the conversation about race relations forever. He helped America to understand that reconciliation isn't about division but addition and about the process of bringing us together as a nation.

Five years after that heroic event, the man who had done more than any other to bring healing to the wounds that separated

1

blacks and whites, who had proposed a revolutionary vision of nonviolent protest, and who had broken the back of Jim Crow laws in the South was taken from us at the height of his powers. The irony of his death—that a man so full of charity and compassion for others would be felled by an assassin's bullet—wounded us all. Yet, his dream did not die. The dream grew larger, and Dr. King became larger than life—such things often happen with prophets. But it didn't stop there, for we're his descendants, and the prophetic mantle he wore now rests on the shoulders of those who would carry forth his legacy to a new generation.

The good news is that the dialogue continues to this day, and the worst kinds of bigotry and oppression are much rarer now than they were a generation ago. African Americans have gained equal opportunity and even equal status in many places. Thanks to the empowerment of higher education and new opportunities in the workplace, we have an aspiring black middle class that was unheard of during those earlier times. Black entrepreneurs head some of the nation's most successful corporations; black educators have tenure at many of the nation's elite colleges and universities; and a generation of black actors, athletes, authors, professors, and politicians has risen to the top of their professions and shown us all what talent and determination can accomplish. It was just this sort of achievement—that "more noble life" he described—that was at the heart of Dr. King's dream.

A LIGHT IN DARKNESS

We no longer have Dr. King to light the way, and many of our self-appointed black leaders seem to be more interested in fostering anger and resentment between the races than in healing division. But we're wiser about such things these days, and a new generation of men and women is coming along who know a race hustler when they see one, and they're not buying it. In most of our urban centers, the black churches are dealing with racial reconciliation in new ways. Most of the time the church does a much better job with complex social issues than the courts or the media. This became clear most recently in the case of the "Jena Six," in Louisiana, where the media managed to enflame a situation beyond the point of reason.[2]

Let me explain. By now everyone has heard that the high school located in this three-thousand-person town had a history of white kids gathering together under a "white tree." Evidently, the southern legacy of racial segregation had been passed on to the next generation. The day after Justin Purvis and company defied the white-only status of this high school hangout by sitting under the tree, they encountered an ominous retaliation—three nooses had been hung from that tree as a terrifying symbol of white power, Jim Crow, and lynching.

The school's African American students gathered under the tree to protest their situation and were surprised that District Attorney Reed Walters essentially made a declaration of war. He emphatically pronounced, "I could end your lives with the stroke of a pen."

Eventually, six black kids from Jena brutally beat up a white youth in response to the escalating racial outbreaks in the city. One of the incidents included a young white boy brandishing a shotgun to assert his racial pride. To the outsider, this looks like a town that has lost its equilibrium. White kids seemed to get patronizing slaps on the wrist—because they are "good kids" at heart, while each one of the "Jena 6" were treated like monsters and were originally threatened with one hundred years in jail for attempted second-degree murder.

Like an unfortunate domestic squabble gone public, the Jena Six problem reveals embarrassing details about this town's racial tensions. "Remember Jena" became a rallying cry for civil rights activists around the nation. In this highly charged atmosphere, copycat nooses were displayed in communities from New York to North Carolina.

Today, the anger and outrage stirred up by the media and out-of-town activists are being replaced by an outpouring of compassion and concern in that small town. The churches of Jena are coming together, with black and white ministers working side by side to repair the damage and create a new spirit of community. Despite the injustices in that case, the black and white citizens of LaSalle Parish, Louisiana, are united by their common bond of faith. In order to find that common ground, they first had to put aside their own prejudice and resentment. They had to recognize that what they had in common was greater than what had kept them apart. If racial healing is attainable in Jena, Louisiana, it's achievable in every other community of the nation.

We're a long way from solving all the problems in society, racial or otherwise, but I would argue that we've also come a long way from the tensions of the 1960s. As a culture, we've learned a lot, and there's much less of the old-fashioned racial hatred in America today than ever before. That's not to say, of course, that discrimination doesn't exist—we all know it does. And it's not to say that there's always fairness in such things as hiring, school and college admissions, criminal sentencing, or the approval of home-loan applications. But we've come a lot further in a shorter period of time than anyone would have believed since Dr. King's assassination forty years ago.

As a pastor who ministers in suburban Washington DC, I've come to see that black and white churches need each other. There's a lot we can learn from each other. It's true that each has a slightly different take on how church is done. We have our differences concerning social justice and community involvement. Neither one has all the answers, but we have many things in common. These things are the truth of Scripture, the doctrine of salvation through faith in the atoning death of Jesus Christ, and the role of the church as salt and light for a world in darkness. The good news of the gospel is all encompassing, and now more than ever believers of all races and denominations need to be working together to spread the good news. This is one of the abiding principles of God's truth in black and white.

FINDING OUR VOICES

The successes of an attractive African American candidate for the office of president of the United States have challenged the claims of those who would have us believe that the days of Jim Crow are still with us. After Barack Obama's victory in the Iowa caucuses in January 2008, syndicated columnist George Will declared that the senator's impressive campaign for the White House signals the end of purely race-based politics in America. I tend to agree, although I admit I was surprised to see that comment in print. Will said the days when black candidates could only count on the support of black voters are long gone.[3] His words proved to be prophetic. In fact, I wrote a Townhall.com article that stated that Al Sharpton and Jesse Jackson were the biggest losers in Iowa, New Hampshire, and beyond.

Senator Obama's support from whites and Hispanics adds further weight to the claim that Dr. King's dream is coming to pass. The historic nature of his candidacy is propelled by the largess of character and charisma of this candidate. Senator Obama is an intelligent, articulate, and able campaigner. He has made a stand with confidence under intense scrutiny. And, on top of everything else, he, his wife, and their two daughters look a lot like TV's Huxtable family. They appeal to both Democratic and Republican voters. But is that really enough to heal such a historic chasm as racism in America?

After Obama's victory in the Iowa caucuses, Rev. Al Sharpton lavished praise on the candidate. But what a change from just a few months earlier when both Sharpton and Jesse Jackson were attacking Obama for "acting like he's white."[4] Both men conducted an angry verbal assault on the senator because he refused to join their tag-team effort to exploit the situation in Jena for political advantage. We are in a season in which true change can occur. Despite Mr. Obama's brilliance, he may be overlooking a foundation building block that could help our nation—the unity of the church. Although he has been accepted by many black church leaders, he has not managed to tap into the power of the evangelical church. The evangelical movement in America is the nation's greatest hope for blacks, whites, and Hispanics to come together. The reason is that we have a common values script—the Bible.

Evangelical churches have concerns about Senator Obama's candidacy; his theology is far from orthodox. His pastor has given praise and honor to Nation of Islam leader Minister Louis Farrakhan and preaches hostility toward whites and Jews from the pulpit.[5] In addition, the candidate has come out strongly in support of same-sex unions and gay-lesbian relationships, and even repudiated the Christian beliefs of one of his strongest supporters, popular Christian musician Donnie McClurkin, who believes that homosexuality is a sin.[6]

It is time we moved beyond stereotypes and started dealing with issues that ought to concern all Americans, regardless of race or social status. We need to make a conscious effort to seek truth and live by it in everything we do. Dr. King reminded us that true Christianity is an active, vital faith. If our faith is only good on Sundays, it's not worth the effort. On one occasion, Dr. King said, "A religion true to its nature must also be concerned about man's social conditions...." And he added, "Any religion that professes to be concerned with the souls of men and is not concerned with the slums that damn them, the economic conditions that strangle them, and the social conditions that cripple them is a dry-as-dust religion."[7]

In my last book, *Personal Faith, Public Policy,* coauthored with Tony Perkins, we focused on issues that a reconciled church can solve. In this book, I will focus exclusively on the practical steps to reconcile the black and white church in the nation. This reconciliation will involve coming to a common vision concerning how we are to solve the problems that the nation faces.

One of the hallmarks of a robust Christian faith is that it teaches us to care for the concerns of others. If we expect to see genuine social reform and policies that really make a difference in our neighborhoods, we will need a short list of social, moral, and cultural priorities that can be understood and supported by blacks, whites, and Hispanics alike. And then we need to take that cultural mandate into the voting booth with us. Historically, black Christians have voted for social justice issues, while white Christians have paid more attention to issues of personal righteousness. Both black and white churches have become a little too comfortable with this "color by number" approach. But that can't continue, and that's one of the central concerns of this book.

A New Faith-Based Alliance

For the past thirty years, Washington's idea of "compassionate conservatism" has looked a lot like social welfare, pouring money into community development programs and charitable organizations without looking too closely at how the work is actually being done. Many black families are still at a disadvantage in our society, and assistance is needed. The number of single-parent homes, broken families, and out-of-wedlock childbirths in the black community is staggering. But government's approach to fixing these things hasn't worked, and there are ongoing questions in many of these top-down programs about accountability and effectiveness. The only way to change habits is to change the heart, and that's not something government can do very well. But it's where the church really stands out.

Throughout this book, I will be dealing with social issues of one kind or another, and my perspective is that there are many things the church can do better than government. Government's advocacy is still needed in some areas, but we need to find ways to transform good ideas into practical solutions that help to lift people out of whatever is keeping them in bondage. Whether it's lifestyle choices, an unwillingness to accept responsibility for bad behavior, or poverty holding some folks down through no fault of their own, blacks and whites can find common ground where we can work together for the sake of the nation and the advancement of the kingdom.

One of the most troubling issues for the black community today is the disparity in enforcement and sentencing for crimes. African Americans know the U.S. justice system isn't color-blind. Too often race tends to be the defining variable that determines the level of justice an individual receives. Here again, Christians are helping to turn things around. Programs such as Prison Fellowship Ministries have introduced the concept of "restorative justice," which makes faith an important component of reform. I will talk about this in more detail in chapter 10. I have witnessed many of the problems with law enforcement firsthand, and I will also mention some of that in these pages. But suffice it to say, there's a need for faith-based public policy to change the way laws are administered and the way justice is being served in our nation.

I also want to speak about ways to lift people out of disappointment and failure. The middle class has quadrupled in size over the last fifty years, and great strides have been made in alleviating the sting of poverty for many black families. Yet, lack of home ownership is still one of the most discouraging aspects of poverty in America. Less than 50 percent of black families own homes today. The church's responsibility to address the plight of the poor is fundamental to biblical faith. From Scripture we understand that God hears the cry of the poor, but we still have problems with poverty, and we can't afford to leave it that way.

Some of the questions we're dealing with are hot-button issues in the political campaigns. Should government give every American free health care? Or should we, instead, have private health savings accounts supported by reduced taxes and incentives? Do we want to risk exposing this nation to the same kinds of problems experienced by citizens of Canada and Great Britain under their National Health Service? A socially active church could make easy work of health-care reform if we ever put our mind to it. By taking an active interest in this issue, our churches can provide an example of Christ's compassion. I will talk more about all these things in chapter 8, where I review the background of today's health-care debates.

Time to Be Heard

I will look at these and other issues, not to accuse or complain, but to raise awareness and to offer commonsense, biblically based solutions to problems that some have described as impossible. Jesus told us that nothing is impossible with God, and I believe that. Every one of these problems can be solved through the loving engagement of men and women in the church today, both black and white. We must all remember that our solutions will empower the church, yet more importantly, they will also heal our secular society. Division, antagonism, or neglect on either side will merely prolong the bitterness and social disunity. Consequently, it is essential that our black-led churches unite with their white brethren to help restore the balance.

A priority at this hour must be to protect the most important institution established by God, the two-parent family, and we can do that now. A federal marriage amendment—debated but never voted on in Congress—is one option. But it is not the only one. In addition, black Christians must join with our white counterparts in speaking out against the holocaust of abortion in this country. And there are other fronts on which we must become engaged. But we must be willing to stand with our white brothers and sisters in order to confront the challenges that threaten all Americans.

At the same time, however, the white-led churches must be willing to embrace our concerns and join with their black neighbors and friends in dealing with the problems our people are facing. When white evangelicals recommit themselves to broadening their cultural horizons, they will find millions of devout black Christians who are willing and eager to join with them to change the face of America.

As we look in greater depth at the importance of marriage and family, criminal justice reform, health-care reform, educational reform, fiscal and economic reforms in our communities, along with other current issues, I hope each reader will be encouraged to become part of the Spirit-led transformation that is shaking the nation today. I am convinced this is a prophetic moment in our nation's history—an earth-shaking alliance of all God's people, of all races, to transform the very nature of society. A great awakening is at hand. Historically, spiritual awakenings have transformed both the people and the culture of our nation. This is not the time to sit by in silence. It is time for the church to rise up and shout, to let its voice be heard and its influence be felt.

It is time for truth in black and white.

■ ■ ■ ■

PART I

THE CHALLENGE OF TRUTH

The New Black Church

O N THE EVENING OF OCTOBER 1, 2004, WE HAD AN ALL-NIGHT prayer meeting at our church on the outskirts of Washington DC, and a young woman named Stacey Campbell from Vancouver, British Columbia, came to speak to us. She had been part of the Toronto Blessing and other outpourings of God's Spirit in Canada, and she came to us with a prophetic word. That message touched all of our hearts, but at one point she turned to me and said, "You're going to prophesy outside the walls of the church. You're going to prophesy to the world about the church."

As you can imagine, I was surprised by Stacey's words. I was moved by all she told us that night, but I certainly hadn't expected any sort of personal reference to my own ministry. But as I reflected on those prophetic words, I recalled that other pastors and teachers had said much the same to me over the last few years on at least seven or eight occasions. Some of them had told me I was going to be on CBS or CNN or the FOX Network talking about the books I have written or things of that nature. But, frankly, Stacey's prophecy seemed like the most improbable thing I'd ever heard.

After the prayer meeting, I went home and had a good night's sleep. But the next morning, as I was preparing my Sunday sermon, I could not help thinking about everything that happened. For some weeks I had been wrestling with my thoughts about the presidential election that was coming in just over a month. So I decided to speak to the congregation about that, and I wanted to share with them a letter I was planning to write to President Bush about some of the problems we have been dealing with in the black community.

The six points I laid out in that letter were the same ones I eventually included in *The Black Contract With America on Moral Values*, which was published in a small, soft-cover edition shortly after Bush's inauguration in 2005.[1] They included:

1. Family restoration
2. Wealth creation
3. Educational reform
4. Prison reform
5. Health care
6. African relief

I spoke to several pastors, including Bishop Eddie Long in Atlanta, Dr. Frank Reid in Baltimore, and several other Christian leaders about the issues I planned on including in the document, and they encouraged me to continue the effort. They felt that the points I covered were the ones that the majority of Christians in our community would see as being the most important. And I felt strongly that if we could get some help in these areas, we could effectively turn the state of black America around.

So I decided I would try to arrange a meeting between the leaders of several of the most influential black churches and the nominees of both major political parties. I live and work in the DC metro area, and I'm not a stranger to the political process in Washington. Since both parties seemed to be serious about attracting black voters, I was pretty sure they would give us an hour of their time. If I could get both Senator Kerry and President Bush to meet with us, each of them independently, we could share our concerns. And we could also tell them that if they expected to win the black vote, they needed to come out in support of these things.

The black vote is substantial and growing all the time, and I felt

certain that the party that demonstrated their willingness to deal
with our issues could virtually be assured of victory in November.
Based on their reactions to the meeting, we would make sure that
word got out to the churches and to Christian leaders everywhere.
I wanted to tell the politicians, "You can be the next president. Are
you willing to work with us?" But, I am sad to say, it didn't work
out as I had hoped.

What happened was disappointing. The Republicans were
anxious to sit down and work with us, but when I went back to
the leaders of the major black churches to set things up, I couldn't
get them to come to the table. They didn't want to be associated
with the Republicans, and many of them told me they were already
committed to the Kerry campaign, even though the Democrats
had not indicated a willingness to deal with our issues. When I
approached the Kerry campaign, they didn't want to be bothered.
They said they had made other commitments, and I got the feeling
they weren't worried about the black vote. They thought they had
it all sewn up.

A Word to the Wise

As I was working on my sermon, I felt a deep sense of conviction
that what I was preparing to preach was what I was supposed to do.
This one sermon was to become the first in a series of messages on
moral choices and how a proper understanding of righteousness
and justice can transform society. I also knew that it was important for me to speak about how our commitment to moral values
should influence public policy. It is not the kind of thing we hear
very often in most churches, but it was a message I felt God was
going to send to the nation. So, beforehand, I told our video people
to be ready.

On Sunday, I preached a message about the responsibility
of believers to live out their faith in the home, the marketplace,
and the voting booth. I said that believers ought to be a force for
righteousness in the culture. I'm convinced that God has given

the black church a prophetic role to challenge the apathy, sloth, and neglect of mainstream America and to awaken this nation to God's truth. The church reacted strongly to my message, and there was an outpouring of the Spirit. Then, at the end of the service, I told the congregation I wasn't going to tell them how to vote. That's a personal matter. But I said that, personally, I was going to support George W. Bush for president because of the moral values he stood for.

"I'm a registered Democrat," I said, "but the Republicans are with us on the key moral issues of our day, and that's why I'm voting for Bush." The next day, as chance would have it, I was scheduled to be on the Trinity Broadcasting Network. I was to be on a nationally televised program along with Bishop T. D. Jakes, Tommy Tenney, and Phil Lutsey. During the program, I was asked to speak a word to the people, so I began preaching as fast and hard as I could about justice and righteousness and all the issues I had just dealt with in my sermon on Sunday. I spoke about the white church and the black church and the problems that have kept us separate, and in the middle of that I felt deeply moved in my spirit.

When the program was over and we were preparing to leave, Bishop Jakes pulled me aside and said, "Harry, you don't need to be preaching that message on TBN. The Christian audience hears what you're saying. You need to give that message to the culture. You ought to be saying that on CBS, CNN, the FOX Network, and other places where that message needs to be heard." In other words, he was saying exactly what I'd already been hearing repeatedly from other Christian leaders, and that really hit home.

It was almost as if we were reading from the same script, and it just blew me away. But then he said, "Here's what you've got to do. You need to start writing some opinion editorials in the major newspapers and get this word out there. It's two weeks until the November elections, and the nation needs to hear from you about this imbalance."

I said, "Thank you, brother. I'll be praying about this." And that's what I did. The next day I enlisted the services of a small public relations firm to help me get the word out. Almost immediately I started getting calls from downtown, and one of them was from Senator Sam Brownback. His office called repeatedly and said the senator wanted to meet with me as soon as possible. He wanted to know more about what I'd said about righteousness and justice and how those ideas have been interpreted or misinterpreted by the political parties.

So later that day I drove down to the Hart Building in DC with my associate, Rev. Derek McCoy, to meet with the senator and members of his staff. He said he had seen me on TBN and was impressed by what I'd said about the need for understanding and reconciliation between blacks and whites. And he was particularly struck by my descriptions of righteousness and justice. So we discussed that in more detail.

I said that righteousness and justice are inseparable in a healthy society. Alone, they don't function properly. They belong together. The senator asked me to define how I was using the words, so I told him righteousness is how we live before God, but justice serves and benefits others. In political terms, as I had said on television, Republicans generally understand what righteousness is about. They know the difference between right and wrong, good and evil, and they know that's important. But they're not as good at the justice stuff, which is the application of righteousness and compassion.

Democrats, on the other hand, tend to have a problem with righteousness. They don't want to think about right and wrong or good and evil. They say it's too difficult to discern. So everything comes down to an issue of justice. The problem is that righteousness without justice leads to hypocrisy. And justice without righteousness means there are no moral standards. Just do whatever you want—or as the Bible says, "...everyone did what was right in his own eyes" (Judg. 17:6; 21:25). And a society that goes that route soon loses its bearings. We ignore our responsibility to others and forget the Golden Rule.

Like Riding a Whirlwind

In the days and weeks that followed that meeting, I noticed that the senator was using my terminology in his speeches in the Senate. And later he even quoted my comments in his book *From Power to Purpose*, published in the spring of 2007.[2] By that time I had written my letter to the president. I listed several steps for bringing about change and renewal, and I was preparing for a private meeting with President Bush. When I met with Senator Brownback, we talked about some of those issues and what it would mean in terms of public policy. The senator agreed that the six issues I had listed were very important. He said it was a visionary document, and he encouraged me to go ahead with my plan to publish *The Black Contract With America on Moral Values.*

No sooner had Derek McCoy and I returned to the car after that meeting than my cell phone started ringing. The first call was from the PR firm I'd just hired the day before, and they said they had sent out an e-mail on my behalf, and the first call they got was from the producers at CBS in New York. I thought that was pretty amazing since we had only started this thing two days earlier. I had just left the Hart Building on Capitol Hill, and here I was getting a call from CBS. Later the same day I got a call from the Christian Broadcasting Network, asking me to come down to Virginia Beach to appear on *The 700 Club.* And that was just the beginning. Suddenly there was a flood of calls from radio stations and television networks all over the country.

It turned out that one of the producers of CBS News had received our e-mail about ten minutes before going into a production meeting, and they were planning on doing a special on the apparent shift in political opinion among black voters at that time. When I heard that, I was stunned. Clearly, this was a God thing, and the pieces were just falling into place.

When I called CBS, I spoke to one of the producers, and he said, "Can you prove to us that you're pro-Bush? Have you endorsed the Republican ticket?" I said I never endorsed any candidate from the pulpit, but I had preached a sermon the previous Sunday in which I told the congregation that I would be voting for the candidate who pledged to support life-affirming, pro-family moral values. And in this election, that would be President Bush.

The next day, we sent copies of the tape from TBN as well as a tape of our Sunday service, and two weeks later they sent a team from CBS News down to DC to interview me. Portions of that interview were used in the special. It was a powerful program, and the network estimated that between seven and a half and eight million people had watched it. I was opposite a black Democratic activist who was against Bush. He argued that John Kerry was the only reasonable choice for black voters, and I laid out my reasons for supporting George W. Bush.

My emphasis, however, wasn't on the man but on the morally conservative Republican platform. The issues the president was talking about were the same ones I had enunciated in *The Black Contract*, and they were in stark contrast to the issues Senator Kerry and the Democrats were promoting. In particular, I emphasized the abortion rate of black babies, and I said it's nothing short of genocide. I said it's crazy for blacks to support any candidate who thinks abortion is a good idea.

That happened on Thursday, and I felt like I was riding a whirlwind. Calls and e-mails were coming from all directions. Then, about ten days after agreeing to the interview with CBS, I received a call from the producer of *The O'Reilly Factor*, and they wanted to know about the black conservative movement. I don't know how they got my name, but I assumed our agent must have been in contact with the producers at FOX. But when they heard that I was scheduled to be on CBS, they suddenly took a big interest in having me on the show, and they worked it out to have me on *The O'Reilly Factor* before the CBS special aired.

I thought that was amazing, but I hadn't seen anything yet. On the day the CBS camera crew came down from New York to do the taping in our Sunday service, a crew from the Christian Broadcasting Network showed up with their own camera crew to tape the same service. So there was CBS on one side of the sanctuary and CBN on the other side. It could have been funny—and nobody was more surprised than I was—but I knew it had to be an act of God. We had a film crew from one of the dominant voices of the secular liberal media on one side of the sanctuary, and another crew from one of the dominant voices of the conservative Christian media on the other side, both of them filming what I had to say.

RENEWING THE DREAM

The next week was relatively quiet, but by the following weekend I was getting calls from radio, television, and print media all over the country. The third weekend I was scheduled to be in, of all places, Montgomery, Alabama, which was the spearhead city of the civil rights movement in the 1960s. That trip had been scheduled weeks earlier, and we arrived on Saturday to get ready for my Sunday morning sermon. Shortly after we arrived, I realized we ought to make a visit to the Rosa Parks Museum, so we changed quickly and drove downtown.

When we arrived, the museum was closed. I felt the need to kneel and pray, so I knelt down in front of the museum with my associates. As I was praying I suddenly felt compelled to stretch out my hands and lie there, to prostrate myself on the pavement. As I lay there, I was praying that God would begin a tremendous work in America.

Something's wrong with our hearts, and there is so much strife and bitterness between the races. The civil rights movement was, from the very beginning, a spiritual movement. It started with a prophetic mandate. As I was praying, the thought came to me that the prophetic mantle Dr. King had worn had never been picked up. Maybe that was because there were actually three aspects to Dr. King's vision for America: the prophetic mantle, a community activism mantle, and a political engagement mantle.

Those are three separate things. The initial influence that mobilized the black church was a spiritual movement of justice that grew out of King's prophetic vision. It was a movement ordained by God, calling His people to live out the true meaning of justice. The civil rights movement took off at that time, not because of the powerful personalities involved, but because this was the issue on God's heart. Because Dr. King spoke prophetically, it became possible for others to continue his work of community activism and political engagement. As I lay there on the pavement at the Rosa Parks Museum, this all became clear to me.

Dr. King was able to operate as a community mobilizer because the civil rights movement struck a nerve. Then, as a community mobilizer, he was given political power and influence to help shape the conscience of the nation. Unfortunately, the leaders who came after him only picked up the community activism mantle. They understood the political engagement aspects, but the engine that ran it, the spiritual mantle, was never picked up.

Driving back to the hotel that afternoon with Derek, I was overcome with emotion. I felt as if the Lord was saying, "OK, Harry, I want you to put feet to this vision. These are My issues. Tell the people what you've seen."

Needless to say, I was deeply affected by the experience and prayed about it that night. The next morning we had a very moving and powerful service. We were in one of the most dynamic churches in the South, and it happened to be the most racially integrated church in the whole area. They told me it was about one-third black, one-third white, and one-third Hispanic. And when I heard these statistics, it was as if God was saying, "Dr. King's dream is actually happening right here in this church!"

Another fact I learned from those folks was even more startling. They told me that the telegraph message that started the Civil War—when Jefferson Davis ordered the first shots to be fired at Fort Sumter on April 12, 1861—had been sent from the Confederate headquarters in Montgomery. The next month, after the Civil War began, the headquarters of the South was moved to Richmond, Virginia. But it struck me that this city had played such a key role in the struggles of our people, from the Civil War and the Emancipation Proclamation right up to the time of Dr. King and the march from Selma to Montgomery in 1965.

In a sense, the Civil War began in Montgomery, and the civil rights movement began there as well. Now, as I was standing in the pulpit of that remarkable church, I felt as if God was going back from beginning to end and healing our history. Dutch Sheets, who is the pastor of Freedom Church in Colorado Springs and is well known for his teachings on prayer, says that God has a way of going back and giving people a chance to repent and redeem themselves from the sins of the past. That's what I saw in Montgomery. And seeing those connections made such a huge impact on my spirit. In that church, on that Sunday, we were seeing signs of even greater things to come.

A Provocative Agenda

On Friday of the following week, I got a call at my office from Ken Hutchinson, who is a gifted black pastor and former pro football player in Seattle. He told me he was working with the May Day for Marriage campaign. Over the past few years they had organized several large rallies and would be bringing 300,000 people to the national mall in Washington DC to take a stand for marriage. Since I live in the DC metro area, Ken asked if I would come and give the opening prayer. Of course I was happy to do that, and I soon found myself down at the mall, praying over this enormous throng of black and white Christians. I understood that this was another part of the work God is doing.

This was such an amazing time for me. From the TBN interview, on October 4, 2004, to the DC Mayday for Marriage Rally on October 15, 2004, it was one of the most moving experiences I have ever had. I was interviewed on approximately fifty-six radio and television broadcasts. Many of the interviews were on secular stations, so the message was getting out there beyond the church. At the same time, dozens of articles were written about the work we were doing, culminating in my op-ed piece in the *New York Sun* on November 2, 2004.[3]

In the editorial, I said it was no accident that a lot of black Christians were planning on voting very similarly to their white evangelical counterparts. Blacks in this country had turned a corner, and we no longer felt that we had to walk in lockstep with the Democratic Party. We didn't have to hold our noses to support the liberal values the Democrats condone anymore. Our people have had a strong moral and religious heritage and have been looking for political leaders who can help us integrate our faith and values with our views about righteousness and justice. And I predicted that this new change of direction would show up in a big way at the polls in November.

That is exactly what happened. As it turned out, it was a small shift in the black vote in Florida and Ohio that turned the tide for George W. Bush and the Republican Party in the 2004 elections. And that's a spiritual story. Right after the elections, when Bush and the Republican candidates had won another squeaker, I sat down to work on *The Black Contract With America on Moral Values*. Ironically, I happened to be on a trip to Hong Kong over the Christmas holidays that year, and whenever I could get some time alone, I worked on that document. It's a simple, straightforward little booklet, but I felt it was a prophetic message laying out the guidelines for a new public policy agenda for the black community.

When *The Black Contract* was complete, we had it published and immediately started sending copies to opinion leaders around the country. Then, on February 1, 2005, we launched our new organization—the High Impact Leadership Coalition. *The Black Contract* provided the operational guidelines for what we hoped to accomplish. At one point a very wise friend took me aside and said, "Harry, God gave you these concepts. You've got to stop waiting for the people to show up who you believe are qualified to talk about it. Stop waiting for the famous black preachers to come on board. Some of them will come, but God gave this burden to you, and you're supposed to carry it yourself."

I heard what my friend was saying, and I felt that was wise counsel. So from there, I flew out to Los Angeles for a meeting cosponsored by Rev. Lou Sheldon and the Traditional Values Coalition. It was held at the Crenshaw Christian Center, where Dr. Fred Price is the senior minister. At first I think some people thought the High Impact Leadership Coalition was a division of Rev. Sheldon's ministry, but we made it clear they were two separate organizations: one made up primarily of white evangelicals and the other primarily of black evangelicals. But we were working toward the same goals.

Some of the church leaders who attended that meeting didn't want to schedule a press conference, because they didn't think the media would show up. We had organized a meeting of forty or fifty black pastors in Washington DC the previous year to address the concerns of Christians about same-sex marriage. That group of pastors represented literally millions of members. They were pastors of megachurches all across America. But the press didn't show up. There was one reporter from the Associated Press, period. We knew why they didn't come: what we had to say about same-sex marriage and the biblical view of sexuality didn't fit the agenda of the mainstream press, so they stayed away in droves.

Much the same thing had happened to us on another occasion when we organized a major announcement concerning support by the black church for the proposed Federal Marriage Amendment. The reporters and photographers ignored what we had to say. Whenever black pastors stand up for traditional moral values and conservative principles, the liberal media looks the other way. If Al Sharpton or Jesse Jackson had been on board with us, you can bet they would have been there. But we were coming at it from a different direction, with a morally and biblically based agenda, and that was simply too provocative for the liberal press.

THE MEDIA RESPONSE

At the meeting in Los Angeles, we were launching a new coalition of African American pastors, and I had a strong sense of calling. On the evening before our first big meeting, my colleague Derek

McCoy and I took a walk in West Los Angeles, and we were praying and asking God for direction. As a sign of His favor, we asked the Lord to put the story of this new coalition on the front page of the *Los Angeles Times*. Now, I knew that was a bold request. In human terms, the chances of something like that actually happening were nil. But that was our prayer, and we never doubted that God could make it happen.

I woke up early, about 5:30 the next morning, and when I opened the door of my hotel room and picked up the newspaper, sure enough there was a story about the High Impact Leadership Coalition on the front page of the *Los Angeles Times*.[4] All six points of *The Black Contract With America on Moral Values* were listed right there on the front page. It really happened, and when Derek and I saw it, we were both praising the Lord.

But the best was yet to come. Because of that front-page story, the press conference we'd scheduled for 10:00 a.m. suddenly went from "Sorry, nobody's coming!" to every major news organization in the country—ABC, CBS, NBC, CNN, AP, Reuters, FOX, and newspapers from all over the world—sitting there in the room, waiting for us when we arrived!

No fewer than two hundred fifty stories and features were published about that event. They were all talking about the black pastors from around the country who had come to Los Angeles to announce the launch of a new coalition of black conservatives. They went on to talk about how the details of a new political agenda are spelled out in a new document called *The Black Contract With America on Moral Values*. They got the message, and God made sure that millions of others would get the message as well.

This started a tremendous buzz all over the country. Some people came out strongly in favor of what we were doing, and there were others who spoke just as strongly against us. In the days and weeks that followed, there were some black pastors who told me that they didn't need a black contract with America, that they were morally conservative and were taking care of their people. But that's what we were saying. We're morally conservative, but we've been supporting politicians who are morally liberal. Now it's time for the black church to speak up and translate what we say we believe into policies we can live with.

A few years ago, Vivian Berryhill, a Mississippi Republican and president of the National Coalition of Pastors' Spouses, presented a document called the Mayflower Compact for Black America. For whatever reasons, that effort didn't seem to get much traction. The document was modeled on the *The Contract With America* by Speaker of the House Newt Gingrich as part of the Republican revolution. Gingrich's document proposed ten new legislative initiatives, from restructuring the federal budget and tort reform to new programs for job creation and term limits. It came at just the right time, and, looking back now at the tidal wave it helped create in 1994, you would have to say it was a stroke of genius.[5]

But every effort of that sort has its detractors, and not every reform package succeeds that well. I realized later that one of the main reasons we made the front page of the *Los Angeles Times* was because another group of black Republicans who had come out to see what we were doing had greased the wheels. These were well-placed folks with a lot of influence in the black community, and I think some of the media people thought we were the same group, and they put the word out. They had a message that was primarily political, while ours was mainly spiritual.

Our contract was based on the three mantles that God had shown me in Montgomery. I understood that we could create a movement for moral and political reform by preaching, and if we could pick up that dynamic, then down the road we could increase the impact of community engagement and political impact. All those things could happen, but for the movement to be successful, there would also have to be an alignment with the spiritual dimension.

There are many places in Scripture where it is clear that God expects us to be faithful to the call, regardless of the consequences. We are not responsible for the results: that's God's job. But we are expected to be faithful to the word He has given us. My job was to speak the words that God had laid on my heart, and then trust

Him for the results. That's where I was. I felt that this was literally the fulfillment of all those prophetic words, when people I greatly respect had told me I was to prophesy outside the walls of the church.

Whenever I stood up at a press conference, I wasn't giving a media briefing; I was preaching. Most of the people in the room wouldn't have thought of it as a sermon, but I was delivering the message I had been given. I think it was fortunate that our message sounded so much like a message that was being whispered in Washington and in boardrooms and newsrooms around the country, that there is a growing backlash in the black community against the liberal agenda of the Democrats and their political base on the left.

AN UNEXPECTED CHALLENGE

Two days after the Los Angeles press conference, I was invited to appear on *The Tavis Smiley Show* on the Black Entertainment Television (BET) network. I felt that was a breakthrough. Tavis had interviewed me on his radio program when I first began speaking about these issues. He couldn't believe that I would call myself a black conservative. To his mind, those words just didn't go together—it was an oxymoron. But whenever they needed somebody to speak from that side of the issue on radio or TV, I was often the one they turned to, and I was getting a lot of media exposure through this.

But right at that point, when it was becoming apparent that an influential minority of black voters had been the deciding factor in the November elections, I was diagnosed with cancer. I had been experiencing discomfort for some time, and I had assumed it was because of the hectic pace of my life. But after an exhaustive series of tests, my doctors gave me the bad news, and that brought with it a whole new set of issues and concerns. Once I began receiving treatments and had a regular regimen of health care, I got back into the swing and continued to interact with the media. But the context was different. Suddenly I was having to think about my own mortality, about the future of my church and my family. And I had to deal with many other things that I had never worried much about before.

More than anything, I believe in the sovereignty and wisdom of God. If He allowed me to contract a potentially fatal disease, I had to believe that some good would come from it. And as I thought about what this diagnosis would mean for me, I had a new sense of urgency about the work I was doing. The word I had received from the Lord in Montgomery wasn't ambiguous at all. It was clear to me that God was at work, taking the work of civil rights and racial reconciliation to a whole new level. There was no way I was going to be unfaithful to that calling.

Furthermore, that message had been affirmed, as I said earlier, at least seven or eight times by pastors and church leaders I respected, men who were walking the walk and talking the talk. I felt the most profound conviction in my soul that the new black church could show America a better way, but for us to be successful we would have to reconsider some of the political choices we had made in the past, and we would have to make sure that from now on our walk would match our talk. In other words, if we preached conservative moral values on Sunday, then we ought to be demanding a conservative moral platform from our elected officials.

Unfortunately, we hadn't been doing that. Too often our community had let the promise of government handouts lure us away from what we knew to be true. And we compromised what we knew in our hearts to be true with what was politically expedient, even though the leaders of our party never lived up to their promises. The politicians discovered they could take our votes for granted so long as they promised us jobs or money or other advantages. When I reflected on all these things, I was burdened by the feeling that we had sold our birthright, as the King James Bible says, for a mess of pottage. (See Genesis 25:29–34.)

We are all going to die sometime, so I wasn't unduly worried about that. As believers in Christ, we have the assurance of life eternal. I knew my future was secure, one way or the other, but I knew that I could not afford to procrastinate, and, if anything, the cancer diagnosis had only magnified my commitment and my enthusiasm for the work I was doing. That, in turn, has prompted me to accept more speaking engagements, more writing and publishing opportunities, and more chances to speak to individuals and groups about our agenda than I could ever have imagined. For however long I have left on this planet, these are issues that I'm compelled to deal with, combating false ideologies and the unwise compromises that conflict with the program of God. And this I know: my assignment has something to do with fulfilling that promise.

A New Moral Mandate

During the run-up to the national elections in spring 2004, a group called Ohio Election Central commissioned a study by the research firm of Market Strategies in Livonia, Michigan, to measure the values of registered voters. What they found was that the black community was predominantly pro-family, against same-sex marriage, and, by a small margin, they supported the aims of the Bush administration. Based on those findings, the organizers realized they needed to get out and talk to black families about the need for a marriage amendment prior to the upcoming elections, and that's what they did.[6]

Having a pro-life, pro-family, conservative moral agenda in the Republican platform, along with a major effort to put though a marriage amendment, increased the overall percentage of black votes and gave a slight edge at the polls to the Bush campaign. In fact, it was just enough to give the Republican Party a victory in the general election in Ohio, which gave them, in turn, the needed margin of victory in the Electoral College.

Evangelicals had been very active in Florida and Ohio during the campaign, and one of the most effective teams was that of

Pastor Rod Parsley, who is a white evangelical, and Ken Blackwell, the black secretary of state for Ohio. The two men traveled the entire state together, talking about the importance of the marriage issue, and thousands of people of all races and persuasions responded to the message.

Subsequently, people like Jesse Jackson and Congressman John Conyers accused the Republicans of dirty tricks and tampering with the vote.[7] They couldn't believe that so many black voters had actually pulled the Republican lever at the polls. But the market study said that black voters would respond to a positive moral message, and in fact they did go to the polls and vote for the president's pro-family agenda. The entire election came down to sixty thousand votes in Ohio, and I'm convinced that was precisely the margin provided by crossover black voters.[8]

Statistics after the election showed that twice as many people in Ohio voted for the Republican ticket in that election than had ever done so before, and there was also a strong correlation between the number who voted for Bush and the number who voted for the marriage amendment.[9] The amendment drew them over, and the fact that the Republicans had established their credentials as the party of traditional moral values was enough to send the president back to the White House with conservative majorities in both houses of Congress.

For decades now, the African American vote has been something the Democratic Party could always take for granted. There are some politicians who truly understand the importance of the black vote and who take it more seriously than that. But there are a lot more who think we are all in lockstep with the Democratic Party and we're never going to waver. Consequently, they don't need to take us seriously, and they don't need to make policy judgments with black folks in mind. Well, I have some news for all those people. Things are changing.

TAKING A MORAL STAND

I'm not anti-Democrat, and I am not pro-Republican. I have been a registered Democrat since I first registered to vote. For many years, I believed the promises made by Democrat candidates who said they wanted to help remove the burden from the backs of black families. I believed they truly wanted to bring needed resources to our communities. But, for the most part, I have been disappointed. I am deeply troubled by the proabortion, pro–gay marriage, tax-and-spend policies of the Democrats. And there are a lot of people in our community who feel as I do. Consequently, there is a new dynamic in our midst: a new surge of African American political activism with strong conservative roots—a movement that is drawing its energy from the conservative moral values of the new black church.

Most of the policies supported by Democrat candidates tend to reflect the values of the party's liberal base. On almost all the issues that matter most to me, I identify more strongly with the platform issues of the Republicans. I am strongly pro-life, pro-family, pro–traditional marriage, and I believe in fiscal restraint and limited government. I have traditional views concerning same-sex marriage and the threats posed by the politically correct "hate crimes" laws sponsored by Democrats. I happen to believe that the Republicans could be doing more to help our people. But how could I continue to support the Democrats when their worldview is precisely the opposite of my own?

More and more African Americans are beginning to question their relationship with the Democrats. If we expect to see real change in our neighborhoods, black voters are going to have to begin taking a closer look at the Republican alternative. And for their part, the Republican Party will have to convince somewhere between 15 and 20 percent of black voters in this country that their long-term interests are best served by Republican candidates who are strong on the issues that matter to blacks. But I am optimistic that, in time and with constructive dialogue, that can happen.

The message that is coming through loud and clear today is that moral choices make a difference, and social policies that undermine our moral choices ought to be avoided. Voting for a party because "we've always done it that way" is no longer acceptable. If we continue to give unwavering support to candidates who advocate left-wing social policies and values that no longer reflect our beliefs, we're only hurting ourselves. But if we align with those who agree with us on issues that truly matter, we will be helping ourselves. And, best of all, we will be taking a stand for righteousness and justice.

■ ■ ■ ■

Tearing Down Walls

I N THE RUN-UP TO THE 2004 ELECTION, I WROTE AN OPINION
piece for the *New York Sun* in which I talked about the changing
dynamics of the electorate and challenged the leaders of both of the
major political parties to take a closer look at what's at stake in the
black community.[1] For decades, both Democrats and Republicans
have tended to ignore the black vote until the last six weeks of the
campaign season. Consequently, we sometimes get the feeling we're
being treated like the other woman in an illicit affair.

We're jostled around from place to place and forced to wait
in the shadows. Promises are made, but few are kept. The politicians are married to others with more money and influence,
yet they always tiptoe back to our door at midnight, whispering
sweet nothings in our ears. Loved only for what we can give, a lot
of black folks are beginning to ask, "At what price have we been
selling our love?"

We are not happy living that way anymore, but I believe things
are about to change. Sophisticated black voters are already beginning to react with disappointment and disgust to the neglect we've
endured with the Democratic Party. At the same time, a new generation of black Christians is emerging, and these people are bold
enough and savvy enough to believe they can do a better job of it
than some of their predecessors have done.

They are tired of listening to empty promises and feel-good rhetoric that produces minimal results. But to make things even more shocking for the political leaders, there is an emerging black middle class made up of professionals and entrepreneurs who have an economically based political agenda very similar to their Republican peers. And these individuals expect to get a better return on investment than they've had so far.

This new voice of black America is helping to call black voters back to basics and away from their adulterous affair with liberal politicians who talk a good game but seldom deliver the goods. The black church has been the primary reference point in the black community for generations, and that's still true. However, the new black church is bigger, bolder, and more dynamic than ever before, and we're speaking out as never before.

CHANGING THE OLD DYNAMIC

The average person in this country probably believes that the black community will always vote for Democrat candidates, primarily for their own personal economic interests. But this is a shallow generalization that takes into account neither the sophistication nor the growing spirituality of today's black voters.

What I have referred to as "the new black church" is outspoken on issues such as same-sex marriage and abortion. Every day and in practical ways, members of these churches are looking at contemporary society with a Bible in one hand and a laptop in the other. Our people have a history of looking to their Christian faith as a coping mechanism, to help them deal with both prejudice and personal adversity. But today we understand that faith is essential in dealing with all aspects of society.

Survey after survey shows that roughly half of all African American adults identify themselves as "born-again Christians." They are more likely than any other group to view their life as a gift from God, and they are the ethnic group most fervent in claiming the promises of God for personal endurance and perseverance.[2]

A poll released in October 2004 by the Joint Center for Political and Economic Studies predicted that President Bush would receive at least 18 percent of the black vote in the 2004 election—which would double the percentage of the 2000 vote.[3] Such findings may be startling to some people, but I have been predicting that at least 20 percent of blacks would be willing to vote Republican for the right candidates and the right issues.

There are two reasons for the shift: the changing needs of middle-class blacks and the deep spirituality of a critical mass of black Christians. The new black church has conservative views on abortion and same-sex marriage, and we are not blind to the fact that the Democratic platform no longer reflects our views. It is no accident that more and more blacks are beginning to think like their white evangelical Christian counterparts about politics. And it is no accident that more and more people in our community are coming to realize that the Reverend Jesse Jackson and the Reverend Al Sharpton don't really speak for us. These are no longer the only voices of black America, and many would say they are not even authentic voices for our people.

The new black church is changing the old dynamic, and we are here to stay. Members of these churches still honor their clergy. They still expect these leaders to help them integrate their faith with contemporary life. But they want their lives and their votes to make a difference, and that means there will be many more changes to come—in our churches, in our homes, and especially at the polls.

If we want to shake up the political apparatus, all we have to do is vote our conscience and make sure that our friends and family know what we're doing and why. We don't have to convince everybody to follow our example. We only have to awaken a thinking core of Christian voters who understand the importance of voting for conservative moral issues. The conservative candidates won't be telling us what our values are: we already have our values. What we want to know is how we can make an impact on the political process, and I'm convinced this is how we begin the process of change.

This is important conceptually because it is a little bit tricky. I believe that what we have to do is to look at the fact that the black community has not received very much for their loyalty over the last forty years. I also believe that this kind of thinking can help the political strategists of the next generation do a better job of serving our needs. When they see that we are watching closely and measuring results, they will understand that they need to take our issues seriously.

There are a lot of folks in the black community who would like to be more active in politics. We feel we have been taken for granted by the Democrats, but it sometimes seems as if the Republicans have already written us off. They say, "We're not going to get their votes anyway, so why are we wasting time?" But I am saying, we are listening now. We are not content with the weak soup we have been given, and we are ready to do business with a party that will take our issues seriously and pay attention to what we are saying.

LISTENING TO THE BASE

Despite the recent controversy over illegal immigration, I have to say that George Bush did an amazing thing because for the first time he got his party to start thinking about the impact of the Hispanic vote. That is an important constituency because, as statistics now show, Hispanics are the largest minority group in the country. Unfortunately, with all the problems over border security and the threat of terrorists coming into this country from Mexico, the president may have shot himself in the foot. But, still, I believe the Republicans have begun to realize that the minority vote is critical to their success.

The administration's focus on this large group of people tells us something about the importance of speaking out. Reform happens when legislators and government officials feel there is enough political capital to be gained by serving our interests. When the black community pulls together to support one candidate, a group of candidates, or a political party, they are doing it because they believe it serves the interests of the community.

Lord Palmerston, who was the prime minister of the British Parliament in the mid-nineteenth century, once said, "Nations have no permanent friends or allies; they have only permanent interests."[4] The leaders of the civil rights movement in the 1960s adopted that phrase because it expressed so well our own situation. And I think it still applies. The black community cannot afford to be wedded to any political groups or individuals forever, but we do have an abiding interest in the public and political issues that determine how we live.

No permanent friends, only permanent interests. The idea is that we will support those who have shown their willingness to act on our behalf. Our interests are for the betterment of the community. We have many problems, that is true. But at heart, the black community has a moral agenda that is driven by our religious values and our desire to strengthen and support the family. And any group of politicians that understands our needs and works to design and pass legislation that supports our values will benefit from our support.

Even if most people assume the majority of blacks are solidly in the Democratic camp, that doesn't mean that a substantial minority of black voters can't make a big difference at the polls. There are some contrarians who are in the Republican camp simply because they want to be different. And there are others I would call political ideologues, and I don't think that is helpful. Over the last twenty or thirty years, politics has become polarized from an ideological stance. Instead of saying, "Here's the problem. Now how do we solve it?" they are saying, "How can we crush the opposition?" Too many politicians today are more interested in stopping their opponents than in serving the interests of their constituents, and that has to stop.

A NEW WAY OF WALKING

In February 2004, I was on *The Tavis Smiley Show*, on the BET network, and during the interview I was asked to discuss my thoughts on what a new paradigm for black voters might look like. I told Tavis and the television audience that my purpose in creating a moral agenda for black voters was to develop a set of public policy priorities that went beyond the standard party fare. It said: "Here's something that black people care about. This is an area of common ground on which we can all agree and which we are committed to support through the political process."

Until now, black voters have not been very good about going into the political process with an agenda. Most of the time we just come up with complaints, because we've trusted people who haven't been very good at delivering on their promises. Time and time again we trust them to take our interests to heart, and they let us down. The unfortunate result in many cases is that a lot of black voters just stay home because they have given up. And there are still a great many black voters who just pull the Democrat lever because, again, "We've always done it that way."

I am not so sure that the old labels of "liberal" and "conservative" even apply any longer. Those terms describe ideologies and worldviews that are not often backed by clear and consistent action. Instead of focusing on specific problems, we take sides with one group or the other and fall into the trap of name-calling. In that atmosphere, otherwise intelligent people end up attacking the motives of their opponents instead of looking at the potential value of the policies they advocate. We cannot afford that luxury anymore.

The test for the black community ought to be, which political perspective will actually create the programs and policies that can make our lives better? What we discover should determine how we vote. Some of the recent campaign debates offer a perfect example of this battle of ideas. We hear speeches about all kinds of approaches, but most Americans are sick and tired of talking about it. We want to see some action. Voters of every persuasion understand that it is in the implementation of their campaign promises that our leaders are letting us down. The politicians don't need a new way of talking; they need a new way of walking.

We have reached the point where words alone aren't enough. Most of the liberal policies we have supported in the past do not work, and for the moment at least there is a new openness to conservative ideas for people in the black community who are serious about making a better life for themselves and their families. This means there is a new generation of voters who are open to morally responsible conservative policies. But that window of opportunity won't remain open for long if the politicians fail to deliver on their promises.

In the yearlong research project I conducted with George Barna, we spoke with a large number of African American pastors who thought like conservatives, not liberals.[5] Unfortunately, their voting records did not line up with their values. In some cases, I felt they had already drunk the Kool-Aid, because they were unwilling to admit that they had been supporting a political agenda that was the exact opposite of what they claimed to believe. They refused to see that the party they had been supporting no longer supported the values they were preaching in the pulpit.

Some of that is to be expected, I suppose. But if we expect to see a renewal of moral values in the black community, we are going to need a new level of honesty and humility from the leaders in our churches. We will need a new breed of Christian leaders who can think "out of the box." They will be entrepreneurial thinkers who are serious about changing the face of their communities. They will not be locked into supporting one party simply because we've always done it that way.

They will preach the old-fashioned, cornbread-and-beans gospel messages, but they will be doing their research and planning with a laptop. They will be savvy enough to know that liberal tax-and-spend policies have done more harm than good to black families. And they will understand that genuine economic empowerment doesn't come with government handouts but with the freedom to determine how we use the opportunities we've been given.

A New Way of Thinking

No doubt this is a new way of thinking for many of our people. But it is essential that we take a fresh new look at our situation and think creatively about how we are going to respond to new opportunities. We hear a lot about the political power of white evangelicals. But in reality, many white churches are still grappling with their role in politics. Some of the more conservative churches speak of politics as "devil's business," or as a breach of the "wall of separation between church and state." Many have been scared off by the ACLU and other liberal groups.

Black churches, on the other hand, expect their leaders to speak out on social issues. We expect our pastors and teachers to talk to us about the morality of certain political issues and to weigh in on the individuals who are coming around asking for our votes. It is true that the political views of many of our black leaders are stuck back in the sixties. They've been shaped by a generation of false alarmists and race hustlers whose interests and tactics no longer apply. But change is coming.

The research George Barna and I published in our book, *High-Impact African-American Churches*, proved that there is an army of thoughtful and responsible African American leaders out there who is not tied to the old stereotypes.[6] They are able to see beyond the racial bigotry and the mistakes of the past and to evaluate political candidates on where they stand on the key issues of the day. It is time for these folks to step up to the plate.

Between 2002 and 2004, I spent a lot of time working on that book. But as we were getting ready to launch the promotion cycle, I found that there were not very many black pastors who felt they needed to know what was in the book. On the other hand, white pastors couldn't figure out why they needed to learn anything from the black churches. There were, however, a number of black church leaders who sat down with me and told me how powerful they thought it was. They felt the book expressed very well the distinctive differences of the black church and explained why our tradition is unique. They said it captured the fundamental dynamics of African American concerns, and since that time I have heard similar comments from quite a few black and white leaders.

But that being said, when we began speaking about our research in the print and broadcast media, I realized we needed to be talking about our findings in political terms. Black megachurches are a relatively new phenomenon, and a lot of people were surprised to learn that the largest churches in virtually every metropolitan area are black megachurches. We have some churches that are larger than even the best-known white congregations, such as Willow Creek in Chicago and Saddleback Mountain in San Diego. By virtue of their size, these black churches can have an enormous impact on the political process.

In metropolitan DC where I live, we have two churches with over twenty thousand members. One church in our area has fourteen thousand in weekly attendance, another has ten thousand, and there are six or seven predominantly black churches with around eight thousand active members. Beyond that, there are a dozen or more with two to three thousand members. Most of these congregations are pastored by people who are not nationally known figures, but they have dynamic and growing ministries.

And that's no accident. Since the turn of the twenty-first century, God has put a hand of grace on the black churches. It is certainly true here in DC, but it's also happening in Atlanta, Dallas, Chicago, Los Angeles, and practically every other large city in the country. Bishop T. D. Jakes, who is a well-known public figure as well as a prolific author and speaker, is pastor of the Potter's House in Dallas, with nearly thirty thousand members.

Just a few miles away is the Inspiring Body of Christ Church, where Pastor Ricky Rush preaches to another large, Spirit-filled congregation. Plus, we have the nationally televised services of ministers such as Bishop Eddie Long and Creflo Dollar in Atlanta, Dr. Frederick K. C. Price in Los Angeles, and others with enormous influence in this country and around the globe. These Christian leaders are helping to usher in a new era and a new way of thinking about the social and moral ills of our day.

A NEW POLITICAL REALITY

Dr. King had a dream for America, and while some black leaders would be quick to disagree with me, I believe that some parts of that dream have been fulfilled. The Voting Rights Act of 1965 has been passed and extended repeatedly by Congress; the landmark case of *Brown v. Board of Education*, which eliminated the old "separate but equal" policies in the schools, is recognized as a milestone of racial justice; the Equal Employment Opportunities Commission and antidiscrimination laws of various kinds have given this generation of blacks the most level playing field in our history. So we have made progress in the right direction.

Personally, I believe that some forms of affirmative action are still needed, but even if affirmative action and race-based quotas were totally eliminated, millions of black Americans have moved into the highest levels of society in business, education, entertainment, government, and every other area. This is not to say that all our problems have been solved, because they haven't. But Dr. King's dream—that one day black and white children would play together and our children would be judged by the content of their character and not the color of their skin—has, to a large extent, been achieved.

Even though there is a lot of work still to be done, it is time for a new dream. But I would argue that it is time for the three mantles of Dr. King's original dream to be restored. Some of our political candidates have been talking about reinventing the dream, but their words are at odds with their performance. By this I mean they talk a good game, but that is not all there is to it.

If we want to see meaningful change, we need to send those people back home and bring in some fresh new faces who understand what we are after. When men and women who value truth begin rejecting the demagogues who don't share our values, we will be able to bridge the racial divide, close the education gap, and shore up the digital divide. And when conservative Christians decide to get behind strong, visionary leaders with genuine faith and a record of commitment, we will be able to defeat radical Islam, terrorism, poverty, and many other problems that may seem impossible to us today.

As I write this, the election of 2008 is rapidly approaching, and we are witnessing one of the most bitterly fought campaigns in living memory. I have never seen so many candidates, from both Left and Right, battling so hard for our votes. They come from opposite sides of the political spectrum, and the rhetoric is more polarized and more extreme than I have ever seen it. One way or the other, this election is going to be a defining moment for the nation. But beyond the race for the White House, which is intense enough, this election will determine who controls Washington for the next four years, and possibly well beyond—and the candidates know it.

Most of the time the political atmosphere in Washington feels like "agenda limbo." Thanks to fallout from the wars in Iraq and Afghanistan, Hurricane Katrina, and other hot-button issues, the Republicans often seem to be gasping for air, while the new Democratic majority in Congress are wielding their newfound power like a bunch of amateurs. They have been so clumsy at it, and their approval ratings, dropping down into the single digits, make it perfectly clear that the voting public is not impressed.

All the chatter about bipartisan cooperation after the midterm elections turned out to be little more than political rhetoric. In less than ninety days, the gloves came off and the power struggles began all over again. We can only hope that the 2008 election will settle the current stalemate in Congress. But whatever happens, both parties will be graded on their performance. The war, illegal immigration, and the economy are major concerns. But we have to wonder, which group will rally and win the hearts and minds of the American people? Who will decide the new political reality in America?

KNOWING WHERE WE STAND

In the 2000 election, evangelical Christians supported George W. Bush, who lost the popular vote, and the election was decided in the Electoral College. In 2004, gay marriage and pro-life concerns woke up a lot of evangelicals. They showed up and voted their values and kept the conservatives in power. In 2006, however, evangelicals were deeply disappointed with the administration's position on immigration and the lack of a clear battle cry concerning the key moral issues of the day, such as abortion, same-sex marriage, stem cell research, and the like. As a result, the Republicans took a beating in the midterm elections, and Democrats were returned to power after more than twelve years in limbo—and then did nothing about it.

Too often in the past, evangelical Christians have fallen into the rut of being defined by what we are against rather than what we are for. In recent months a lot has been written about the waning influence of evangelicals in the political arena. I think a lot of the press coverage is wishful thinking, however, with many in the liberal media hoping these true believers will just "go back to church." But no matter how much they wish it, the Christian electorate isn't going away anytime soon.

Conservative Christians have a theology of social involvement that has been preached in one form or another for over thirty years. In addition, there are tens of thousands of young people preparing to enter the public square at schools as diverse as Liberty University and Harvard Law School, and they are steeped in the conservative political tradition. For these reasons, I believe the influence of the pulpit will continue as a strong influence in the political process. And nowhere is that more certain than in the new black church.

The question of the hour, however, is what will this army of voters do at the polls? Will the evangelicals find their voice in the next election? Or will the Republican defeat in the 2006 midterm elections give the evangelical community social laryngitis? I believe the days of blind allegiance to one party are coming to an end. Evangelical leaders are well aware of the failings of both political parties, and we know where we stand. I believe that black and white conservatives, both together and independently, are going to advocate for culturally transforming policies that will reshape the political landscape. They will also shun the image of being mean-spirited spoilers. After all, the word *gospel* does mean "good news."

A PRACTICAL AGENDA

This is why I drafted a series of political issues that can have significance for this new generation of black and white Christian voters. The first initiative I have addressed is easily the most important: family reconstruction. In essence, this means rediscovering the importance of marriage and family and rebuilding this most essential institution with the aid of political and domestic programs that encourage marriage, family formation, and nurturing our children in traditional two-parent homes. Nothing is more important to the future of the black community than a renewed emphasis on families and the moral and emotional fitness of the next generation.

The next is wealth creation, which comes in many forms. The black church has played an important role in neighborhood enterprise, community renewal, and the development of innovative programs to encourage home ownership. Many of our churches offer microfinancing options for home ownership, and that's an important new trend. But we also need legislation to simplify the tax code and provide the kinds of economic stimulation to black communities that will allow more black families to move into the ranks of the middle class.

The third agenda item, educational reform, is vital to the success of the next generation of African American youth. I will deal with each of these issues in more detail in later chapters, but nothing is more important than creating an environment in our homes and communities that rewards and encourages educational attainment. This is an area where I can offer a personal testimony: without the support of my family and my father's decision to provide me with a first-class education, I would not be doing the work I am doing today. As a community, we need to find ways to make it possible for more of our children to get the quality education they deserve.

Prison reform is perhaps our most challenging dilemma, but it is one that affects every black community in America. As I will discuss later, African Americans bear a disproportional share of the burden, and the sentences given to black offenders are longer and generally harsher than those given to white and Hispanic criminals. Statistics bear this out. There are a number of private programs and some outstanding Christian ministries devoted to this issue, and there are models for making needed reforms. But government needs to listen to our concerns, and we need to find an apparatus for achieving balance and fairness in this area.

Health-care reform has been hotly debated since at least 1994 when Hillary Clinton first proposed a national once-size-fits-all program for nationalized medical care. Mrs. Clinton and her supporters described the plan as federally funded health insurance for everyone. But as voters learned more of the details, they realized it was another version of the National Health Service programs that have been such colossal failures in Canada and Great Britain. Those initiatives, funded by higher taxes, subject even seriously ill patients to shockingly long waits, hasty and incomplete diagnoses, and inferior treatment by doctors who are underpaid and overworked.

Socialized medicine is not the answer for the medical needs of the black community; however, federal and state governments do need to reconsider how they can help the millions of men, women, and children in our community who deserve quality medical care but can't afford the high cost of health insurance. This means that a new kind of creative thinking and cross-pollination between government, private citizens, physicians, and health-care providers will be needed. Lowering the costs of health care for families and providing some sort of safety net for those at the lower end of the scale would be a great beginning.

African relief is the last of the six issues in the black contract, and not an issue that immediately comes to mind for many of us. But when we see the images of suffering children in Africa, we know instinctively that something has to be done. African Americans, in particular, should have an interest in helping those who are living and dying today in the lands of our ancestors. The Bush administration has made a good start, with grants of more than $48 billion in financial assistance for the treatment of HIV/AIDS victims in Africa.[7] But even that may not be enough.

We have seen several new programs where government and private charities are working together, and the government has sent scores of physicians, sanitation engineers, and experts in agriculture and natural resource development to help improve standards in those places. But a lot more needs to be done, and it is only fitting that African Americans should take a leading role in helping to bring hope and transformation to the hurting peoples in the third world. It is something we cannot, in good conscience, ignore.

THE NEW BLACK POWER

Black conservatives come in many shapes, sizes, and party affiliations. Perhaps this is a perfect time for wise conservatives to start building bridges with the leaders of the new black church. Even though our people have supported the Democrats for generations, we are what I would call classical social conservatives. By that I mean we believe that government programs alone cannot eliminate crime and poverty. Government alone can't improve the quality of our schools. But government can help create an environment in which constructive changes can take place.

The new black church isn't hanging around, waiting for a handout. We are promoting change through wiser, biblically informed choices and a renewed emphasis on personal accountability. We don't need marches or riots to achieve our goals. What we have in mind is a new kind of black power to transform the nation through the power of faith. We believe we can change America because we know the power of personal transformation through religious conversion. And we know the potential for community transformation through education and economic development.

White conservatives and especially evangelical Christians will have to learn some new methods if they expect to advance their agenda. If they expect to protect America against a deluge of bad liberal policies, they will need to make bridge building and coalition formation with black conservatives a priority. And that would be the smart thing to do.

Not long ago I was interviewed on a national broadcast along with three leaders of black megachurches. These men are the voice of the new black church in America. They are leaders of churches with active membership from fourteen thousand to twenty-four thousand, and each of them supervises community-building programs that have transformed their communities. What they've learned about the power of faith and practical compassion can be replicated all across America. And I believe that knowledge can transform the nation.

The pastors were Dr. Floyd Flake of New York, Pastor James Meeks of Chicago, and Bishop Eddie Long of Atlanta. These men represent a "civil rights" revolution that is very compatible with the goals of the conservative movement. Dr. Flake served as a United States Congressman from New York for eleven years. During that time, he never forgot that he was called to serve the needs of his own community. He never let partisan rhetoric obscure his vision of a faith-based approach to serving his constituents.

On many important issues, Dr. Flake stood with Republicans— to the chagrin, no doubt, of his Democratic Party colleagues. But he was determined to put policy over politics. Over the years he and the members of his church helped to build more than six hundred homes in Queens, New York. During the 1980s, large sections of the borough were drug-infested ghettos, but today this area includes some of the nation's most affluent neighborhoods.

Since leaving Congress, Dr. Flake is still serving the people as president of Wilberforce University in Ohio and senior pastor of Allen Temple Church. This is a man who understands God's calling for the new black church.

James Meeks, who is pastor of Salem Baptist Church in Chicago, spoke to the TV audience that day about when he took three hundred church members down to a drug-infested neighborhood and singled out one crack house to pray over. These bold spiritual warriors stood on the street, stretched out their hands, and prayed that the crack house would close down and the leaders would be converted.

It seemed like an outrageous prayer to the onlookers. Things like that just don't happen. But, lo and behold, a couple of years later, a man came up to Pastor Meeks after a church service and identified himself as the owner of that crack house. He said he had been converted, and he now attends Bishop Eddie Long's church in Atlanta, which happens to be one of the five largest churches in America and a congregation with a dynamic community outreach. You can just imagine how that man's testimony touched the members of Pastor Meeks's church and how one man's change of heart affected an entire community.

For his own part, Bishop Eddie Long has encouraged business development among his members for many years. Through microfinancing initiatives and local workshops concerning home ownership and wealth building, Bishop Long and his staff have trained people to be good stewards of their personal resources, as well as godly mothers and fathers and community leaders. When I visited that dynamic church for an in-house men's ministry event, I expected a crowd of perhaps one hundred people. To my surprise, the men's fellowship had more than three thousand men in attendance on a Saturday morning, listening to messages designed to strengthen their roles as fathers and husbands.

A RECORD OF SUPPORT

This is why I say that these churches, and thousands like them all across the country, can literally change the landscape of America. The black power movement of the sixties was built on cruelty and rage. In the end, the movement created more enemies than friends and failed to accomplish any of its stated goals. The power of faith, on the other hand, can change the way we do business and the way we do politics, and it can even bring political parties back to the moral high ground. It has happened before. And this is the legitimate way to make our voices heard.

To be sure, church leaders are not the only ones doing the Lord's work in our communities. There are thousands of laypersons in black-led churches, who represent millions of members who are making a difference. These are people who want to see changes in their communities. They want to see renewed vitality and integrity in their homes, and they want to see a new birth of righteousness in their schools, businesses, and in the nation as a whole. And they are making it happen by putting feet to their dreams.

When these Christian warriors see how poorly they have been represented in the past, they realize that the old ways have failed us and need to go. The rhetoric of the Jesse Jacksons and Al Sharptons needs to go as well. And there needs to be a new spirit of reconciliation between black and white Christians who share a common interest in rebuilding the moral foundations of the culture.

Can this really be done? I believe it can. The strong showing in my own home state by Lieutenant Governor Michael Steele in his 2006 bid for the Senate showed that leaders of the new black church are willing to support conservative candidates with a record of support for pro-family, pro-life, and other morally conservative issues. Steele's candidacy also showed that black voters will pull the Republican lever for candidates who take a clear stand on moral policy issues.

At the height of Steele's campaign, several pastors of predominantly black megachurches bravely endorsed him, even though this meant they would be opposing a Democratic candidate. These same leaders even took to the airwaves in a get-out-the-vote campaign on radio and television in our area. I'm sure it wasn't the easiest thing for them to do, but they were willing to take a calculated risk by supporting the Republican candidate because they believed it was the right thing to do. Lieutenant Governor Steele had shown that he was the only moral conservative in the race, and even though he lost the race, his supporters believed it was worth the effort.

DEALING WITH ADVERSITY

Am I saying that changing horses and changing direction will be easy? No, of course not. Genuine reform is never easy. However, this book has been written for people who recognize the risks and the potential rewards of taking a bold stand for righteousness and justice. I'm writing for those people who aren't satisfied with the status quo but who are willing to begin a process of change that can lead to greater peace and satisfaction in our world. My own perspective is that of a Christian pastor and author, but I understand that there are people—both Christian and secular—who come at these issues from an entirely different direction.

In that light, let me offer a personal story that may help clarify my point of view. A few years ago my brother, Eric, and I dropped our mother off at the airport in Dayton, and we were headed back to Cincinnati, where we had grown up, in a late model green Cadillac. We were driving through a rural part of the state and had just passed through an area where there's a big outlet mall, when we realized we'd run over something in the road and the car had a flat tire. So we pulled over to the side of the road, and we got out to see what had happened.

As Eric was checking the tire, I got out on the passenger side to stretch my legs, and all of a sudden four police cars pulled up behind us. Not one police car, but four of them—two state troopers and two local sheriffs. They hadn't come to give us a hand, and they obviously didn't come to chat. Instead, they immediately crouched down behind their car doors with guns drawn. When I saw that, I put my hands in the air and said, "Eric, turn around slowly, and keep your hands visible."

Eric was on his knees checking the tire, and he was exasperated that his brand-new car had a flat. So without looking up, he said, "What are you talking about?" I just repeated, "Eric, get up slowly, and put your hands up where they can see what you're holding." He still had his cell phone in his hand, but one of the officers came closer to check us over, and we explained what we were doing.

I told them I was a pastor, and we were on our way home from the airport when the car had a flat tire. After they checked our IDs, the troopers told us they had just gotten a call on the police radio that two guys had been in a fight at the mall, and one of them might be carrying a weapon. So when they saw our car stopped beside the road, and these two well-dressed black guys standing around it, they thought we might be the ones they were looking for.

It was upsetting and embarrassing, but they soon realized that we weren't the guys they were after, and they got back in their cars and went on their way. When they left, they didn't apologize. They didn't say they were sorry for scaring us like that, with drawn weapons, or giving us the third degree. They just got back in their cars and left. They were white. We were black. And I still remember the sense of frustration and humiliation I felt.

I should also mention that this part of southern Ohio has experienced a lot of racial unrest over the years—there had been a couple of race riots in Cincinnati a week or two earlier, which happened to be right before the 2004 elections. As everyone knows, it turned out to be a close and heated election. The Ohio Republican Party was asking blacks to support the ballot for a marriage amendment that would define marriage as the lawful union of a man and a woman. And this meant that people who hadn't always been on the best of terms with whites in that state, and who had their doubts about white Republicans in particular, would have to cross over to vote for the Republican ticket.

But here's the most remarkable thing: despite the divisions between blacks and whites in Ohio at the time, the amendment was important enough to the black community that they voted in record numbers for George Bush and other Republican candidates. In the end, it was the black vote in Ohio that gave the election to the Republicans. And they were able to get black voters to swing from the Democratic Party to the Republican Party because of the strong appeal of the pro-marriage, pro-family, and pro-life moral issues they stood for.

COALITION BUILDING

The message that went out to the black voters in Ohio was crafted to point out just how important it was to elect candidates who shared our moral values. Ohio Secretary of State Ken Blackwell, who is a pro-family black conservative, traveled all over the state with Rev. Rod Parsley, who is a white evangelist. Together, they stressed the importance of a unified voice on these critical social concerns. It turned out to be a dynamic partnership, with a black politician and a white pastor working together for the common good. And, clearly, it worked.

Incidentally, Ken Blackwell is a Republican, but Rod Parsley is an Independent. He says he supports mostly Republican candidates because of their stand on the important moral issues, but he's not wedded to the GOP. And I think that is a principled position to take. There are many Republicans who used to believe that their party could do no wrong, but since the 2004 election, the president and the Republican Party have taken some controversial stands on immigration, border security, and the North American Free Trade Alliance (NAFTA) that may have shattered the unity of the party. Consequently, there are a lot more people who share Rod Parsley's reservations and who are now calling themselves Independents.

There is no question that the marriage amendment was an important issue for the black community, and Ohio voters passed a version of it in that state. I truly believe George Bush was reelected because of that one issue. But then, to their shame, the national GOP backed away from the Federal Marriage Amendment in the 2006 election, and we now know the result. Without that strong coalition of values voters, the Republicans lost both the House and the Senate.

The president's immigration policies were part of that as well. Many people who were angry that President Bush steadfastly refused to secure the borders and seemed to be turning a blind eye to the flood of illegal immigrants coming into the country simply stayed home. In some cases, disgruntled voters actually undermined their own party by voting for the opposition. The GOP couldn't have done a better job of shattering the unity of the party if they had tried, and who knows how or when that coalition of values voters will come together again.

I believe it is essential to establish a solid conservative coalition across denominational, political, and racial lines. The issues we are dealing with today are too important not to do it that way. My approach in this book is meant to be broad enough for all of those groups to embrace, whatever their philosophical or political position may be. But having said that, I believe in a strong moral stand because it is validated by the Scriptures. There is no question that Dr. King did it that way. He knew that righteousness and justice could be achieved because God had said so in His Word, and I want to follow that model as well.

The first premise is that we need a specific vision—a dream, if you will—for what we hope to achieve. It is a vision that we can articulate in specific areas, and those are what I describe in *The Black Contract With America on Moral Values*. But if you look at the issues that have been foremost in the presidential debates and in the political process in general, very few of these issues show up. Poverty has been addressed as a generic problem of the black community. Democrats continue to talk about it and to campaign on this issue, but there are never any concrete steps for ending the scourge of poverty in our neighborhoods. The promises are there, but nothing ever changes.

The challenge before us, then, is to reflect on where we are today, to make a judicious reappraisal of where we have been, and then to look ahead to where we want to be in ten, twenty, or thirty years from now. Then we must do whatever it takes to get there. Ultimately, that will mean building a new coalition of values voters and crossing over to new ground. And it will also mean tearing down some old walls.

■ ■ ■ ■

Civil Rights and Wrongs

THE TRUTH IN BLACK AND WHITE IS A TWO-EDGED SWORD. It cuts both ways, and sometimes what it reveals is hard to acknowledge. Over the years we have come up with all sorts of dodges and mental gymnastics to help us avoid looking too closely at the truth, but we are not going to be doing that in these pages. In this chapter, I want to deal with some issues that many people would prefer to avoid or simply ignore. But if we hide our eyes from the truth, then we will never get beyond the problems that have plagued our communities, and we will never be able to bridge the chasm that separates us from the rest of society.

For decades now African Americans have struggled with the problems of single-parent families and broken homes. Poverty, crime, out-of-wedlock births, abortion, and drug abuse thrive in many of our neighborhoods. Sociologists tell us that the single most troublesome issue facing the nation today is the breakdown of the two-parent family, and nowhere is this problem of greater concern than in the black community. In the late 1940s and 1950s, more than 80 percent of all children in the black community were born to married couples. Over the last fifty years, that figure has been turned upside down, to the point that today as high as 70 percent of all children born to African American women are born out-of-wedlock.[1]

So what is the impact of all these dramatic changes? The answer is that the loss of parental authority, and particularly the absence of a father's influence in the home, has had serious and long-term consequences, including a startling rise in crime and violence. This is not theory but a proven fact. The correlation between family breakdown and juvenile crime is spelled out in a major study conducted by Dr. Patrick Fagan and associates at the Heritage Foundation in Washington.[2] Through a systematic analysis of national crime data, researchers were able to pinpoint the connections between broken families and the crime rates in urban centers all across America. Here's a sample of what they found:

- Since the 1960s, the rise in violent crime parallels the rise in families abandoned by fathers.
- High-crime neighborhoods are characterized by high concentrations of families abandoned by fathers.
- State-by-state analysis reveals that a 10 percent increase in the percentage of children living in single-parent homes leads typically to a 17 percent increase in juvenile crime.
- The rate of violent teenage crime corresponds with the number of families abandoned by fathers.
- The type of aggression and hostility demonstrated by a future criminal is foreshadowed by unusual levels of aggressiveness as early as five or six years of age.
- The future criminal tends to be an individual rejected by other children as early as the first grade who goes on to form his own substitute family, often the future delinquent gang.

For years now, liberals and some of the old warhorses of the civil rights movement have insisted that the biggest problem facing

African Americans today is racism. Nobody would ever say that it doesn't exist—we have all been exposed to racism in one form or another. But the problems caused by racism and bigotry don't even come close to the problems caused by family breakdown and the lack of a father in the home. Several recent studies have shown that problems such as teen pregnancy, drug abuse, dropping out of school, and juvenile crime are more closely correlated with father-lessness than any other social factor.

A study conducted over several years, simultaneously in this. country and New Zealand, found that the incidence of teen pregnancy was highest in single-parent homes headed by a female. The study, published in the journal *Child Development*, concluded that it doesn't matter whether the teenager in such a home is rich or poor, black or white. It doesn't matter if the teen was born to a teenage mother or to an adult mother, or even whether or not she was raised by parents in a dysfunctional home environment. The greatest single factor in determining whether or not she will become pregnant before marriage is whether or not there is a father present in the home. In other words, young women are much less likely to be looking for love in all the wrong places if they know that Daddy is around.[3]

In another study reported in the *Journal of Marriage and Family*, researchers found that the presence of a father in the home was five times more important in predicting teen drug use than any other factor, including income and race. A Harvard report combining the results of four major studies found that children without a father in the home are twice as likely to drop out of school or to have to repeat a grade, as children who live with their fathers. Even more eye-opening is a study published in the *Journal of Research in Crime and Delinquency* that found that children of poor and wealthy families have similar juvenile crime rates when there is a father in the home.[4] What this says is, it is not about the money, and it is not merely about racism; it is whether or not there are reliable standards and some form of consistent moral discipline in the home.

SETTING THE RECORD STRAIGHT

The greatest predictor of poverty isn't discrimination; it's family breakdown. And the greatest contributor to the moral chaos we see in the inner city today isn't slavery or white racism. It's the fact that millions of young people in the black community are trying to get along without moral standards or a strong male authority figure in their lives. Many young people have been told that all their problems come from outside the neighborhood, when, in fact, our greatest handicaps are mostly self-inflicted. There is a tendency among teenagers, both black and white, to think that premarital sex is cool, harmless, and risk free. But that is not true. All too often the godly counsel that helped our parents and grandparents walk the straight and narrow path has been lost, ignored, or conveniently forgotten.

To illustrate how much things have changed in a relatively short period of time, a researcher at Johns Hopkins University in Baltimore pointed out that black children were more likely to be raised by both parents during slavery days than they are today.[5] These are disheartening facts. But in light of these findings, we have to wonder if there is any hope of turning things around. To this, I would have to say yes. Furthermore, in some places, the turnaround is already taking place. In that regard, the Heritage Foundation report cited above offers some encouraging news.[6] What the researchers found was that:

- Neighborhoods with a high degree of religious practice are not high-crime neighborhoods.
- Even in high-crime inner-city neighborhoods, well over 90 percent of children from safe, stable homes do not become delinquents. By contrast, only 10 percent of children from unsafe, unstable homes in these neighborhoods avoid crime.
- Criminals capable of sustaining marriage gradually move away from a life of crime after they get married.

- The mother's strong affectionate attachment to her child is the child's best buffer against a life of crime.
- The father's authority and involvement in raising his children are also great buffers against a life of crime.

Analysts looking at the glaring disparity in crime rates between blacks and whites in this country tended at one time to believe that race was the main cause of crime. That was a dangerous stereotype then, just as it is now. But the Heritage Foundation study reveals that the stereotype was false. What the data actually show, they said, is that the primary predictor of crime isn't race but family structure, along with the nature of the relationship between fathers, mothers, and their children. Simply stated, the greater the number of broken homes and single-parent families in the community, the greater the risk of violent crime.

The incidence of broken families is higher in the black community, and, believe it or not, some people apparently think this is a good thing. I recently saw an article in the *Washington Post* that said that more and more young women today have decided that marriage is not fashionable. It is unnecessary at best, they say, and old-fashioned at worst. The writer of the article cited the comments of a group of twelve-year-old girls who told her matter-of-factly, "Marriage is for white people."[7] I suppose that this shows a new way of thinking.

Unfortunately, based on the marriage rate in the black community today, those young women appear to be right. As the writer of the article reports, the marriage rate for African Americans has been dropping since the 1960s, to the point that today blacks have the lowest marriage rate of any ethnic group in the country. According to official census reports, 43.3 percent of black men and 41.9 percent of black women in the year 2001 had never been married. By comparison, this was true for only 27.4 percent of white men and 20.7 percent of white women. Today African

American women are the least likely group in America to get married. Between 1970 and 2001, the marriage rate in this country declined by 17 percent for all Americans, but it was double that for blacks, falling by 34 percent.[8]

Part of the fallout of these statistics shows up in the extremely high abortion rates for black mothers, as well as in the inordinately high rates of out-of-wedlock births. In addition, sociologists Douglas Smith and Roger Jarjoura, in a study of 11,000 individuals, reported that "the percentage of single-parent households with children between the ages of 12 and 20 is significantly associated with rates of violent crime and burglary."

This study makes clear that the assumption there is an association between race and crime is false. However, since out-of-wedlock childbirth is a major concern of the black community, that places the brunt of the problem of juvenile crime squarely at our doorsteps. It is the absence of marriage and the failure to form and maintain intact families, researchers tell us, that explain why violent crime is out of control in so many of our neighborhoods.[9]

TURNING THINGS AROUND

It's amazing what we can accomplish when we decide to get involved, and there are so many ways that concerned Christian people can make a difference. We don't have to accept these sobering numbers, and we don't have to be stuck with the social pathologies that are eating away at our neighborhoods. Spending time with a child from a single-parent home—taking a boy to a baseball game, mentoring a teenage girl who needs some fatherly advice or just some one-on-one attention from a caring adult—can make such a big difference. So many of our young people are crying out for attention and moral guidance. It may take a little time out of your week, but these aren't hard things to do, and the payback is incredible. You will make a difference for that young person, but you'll be blessed by the experience in ways you can't begin to imagine.

We talk a lot about the need for change. Well, this is change we can make on our own time through personal involvement. We certainly want to be involved politically, to vote for the right people, and to keep an eye on the kinds of policies our elected officials are giving us. But for there to be meaningful and lasting change, there also has to be a commitment to the people who live next door, or down the street, in our own communities.

What's the payback for making these kinds of changes? There are forces in American society that have fomented disrespect if not outright hatred for this country and its history. Some of it may have been well-meaning, because of the legacy of slavery and our inability to completely eliminate inner-city poverty. But some of it has been motivated by partisan politics. Without naming names, I would say that some of our politicians felt that they had to turn our frustration and anger on a common enemy in order to rally their troops and build a political following. For some of them, the enemy of choice turned out to be the American people, or at least those people who didn't subscribe to their political vision.

But that sort of mentality has hurt us, because if we hate our country and its institutions, then we will not have the desire to protect and preserve this nation when we are threatened by enemies, foreign and domestic, who can do us real harm. If we allow ourselves to hate our fellow citizens, then we're going to be divided as a people and at war in our own homes.

There are a lot of young people who have seen the failed values of their parents' generation, and they want their world to be different. I think that this is a hopeful sign. In rejecting the selfishness, the hypersexuality, and the irresponsibility of the previous generation, our kids are actually crying out for meaning and maturity. There are several recent surveys that confirm the changing attitudes of young people. But our children also need to understand that hating other people and other races, or hating our country and its institutions, is not the answer. Instead, they need to recognize that we have problems and then try to find places where they can make a contribution.

What I believe a lot of young people are reacting to is that, whether we like it or not, conservatives tend to come off as self-appointed naggers and complainers. They want to be the conscience of the nation. The hypocrisy and double standards of some of our leaders, saying one thing and doing something else, is part of the motivation behind the attacks on our traditions.

Not too many years ago I used to hear conservatives talking about "the faith of our fathers." Knowing that there were slave owners among the founders of this country and people who had done all sorts of reprehensible things, I began to think about how phony our nation's fathers had been and how all these conservative hypocrites were trying to rebaptize their history into something it was not. But my perspective, I later learned, was the view of someone who hadn't truly grappled with the facts. I had believed what I had been taught by teachers who, I came to realize much later, had a racial agenda of their own.

A Timely Warning

The more God helped me get over my resentment of these people who were defending the traditional culture, the more I began to understand that there truly was a heritage and a tradition that make sense and are worth defending. I was basing my feelings about that tradition on the lack of compassion I saw among some of the most conservative folks—meaning that I looked at people like the Moral Majority and others with suspicion. I have only myself to blame for that.

For many years the Moral Majority was headquartered in Lynchburg, Virginia, and I remember hearing some people say that the town got its name because they had lynched so many black people there. Of course, that is not true. The town was named for the first settler, John Lynch, who operated a ferry on the James River. But that is how strong the resentment was among a lot of people at the time.

When people are bitter about what they perceive as prejudice and disrespect from other people, they will descend into that type of cynicism and in the process become guilty of holding a type of racial prejudice that is just as bad as the prejudice they are criticizing. But, even so, I am afraid the liberal element in this country has taken that direction with shameless abandon. Name-calling, invective, and slander may not be the only way they know how to deal with their opponents, but they found they could always get a crowd by doing it that way.

But there is a further warning, not just to our community but also to the nation, that needs to be heard. The family breakdown we see in the black community today is a prophetic picture of where the entire nation is going to be in twenty years if something doesn't change the trajectory. The collapse of the family structure in black America is where this country is headed unless something brings about a change of heart and a new consensus on the most basic moral values.

In the book *Mismatch: The Growing Gulf Between Women and Men*, Andrew Hacker writes that the makeup of white families is going the same way that black families went back in the 1960s.[10] As late as 1960, 67 percent of black households were headed by a husband and wife, compared to 90.9 percent of whites. But by the year 2000, the figure for white families had dropped to 79.8 percent, and births to unwed white mothers went from 2.3 percent in 1960 to 22.5 percent in 2001.[11] So the pathology is already there. It's not too hard to imagine that changes of this magnitude could one day lead to the utter collapse of the American culture as we know it.

Washington Post journalist and TV commentator Juan Williams has written about Bill Cosby's comments concerning some of the disturbing trends in black culture. In his book *Enough*, Williams says that, essentially, the famous comedian was trying to say that we need to take care of our own families, prioritize education, and learn to be more conservative in financial matters.[12] I'm sure Bill Cosby is not a political conservative since he has spoken out many times on behalf of liberal social policies. But if that's not a basic conservative message, I've never heard one. Personal responsibility and financial conservatism are bedrock principles of the conservative movement.

The issue is that, in general, blacks haven't taken ownership of their own destiny. The sin of the handout mentality that emerged in the sixties was that it weakened the willpower and resolve of many of our people. But that's where Cosby gets beat up by the media and the political establishment. What he was saying runs counter to the standard liberal mantra of the last forty years.

There are three things about Cosby's message that need to be mentioned. First, he was the symbol of achievement back in the days of his comedy routine and the *I Spy* era. He was very popular with blacks and whites and put a good face on our community, but during that time he refused to speak out on social issues. That was probably a wise decision, because his very presence was groundbreaking and powerful. It made people look at blacks in a different way.

So as a public figure, he served us well. By the time we got to the Huxtables and his role as a family man, he also gave us a visual picture of what an intact, middle-class black family could be like. That was certainly commendable. His detractors, however, pointed out that he had had problems with women. The news media squashed that right away, but it came back again, along with the fact that he was a womanizer who had been accused of some very questionable behavior.

Yes, that is his private life, and one could argue that his behavior wasn't all that uncommon for actors of his era. But knowing all that, many people felt that for him to suddenly get up on his high horse, attacking the way our people behave and saying all these things about family and marriage, was offensive. His comments made headlines around the world. He was saying that people need to learn about parenting, they need to prioritize education, and they need to be financially responsible. We don't need to be giving our kids hundred-dollar gym shoes. They need to be spending more time on homework, which is all fine and good. But some of the leaders in our community felt like Cosby was disrespecting our people, and worse, he was airing our dirty laundry in public, and that was unforgivable.

Rejecting the Messenger

When people like Jesse Jackson and Cornel West came out on the attack, they said they were insulted by the way Cosby said it. I was on a panel with Cornel West in 2005. As you might guess, we hold very different views on most things. But after the conference was over, he said to me, "You know, I don't agree with you on a lot of stuff. But I want to tell you something about your attitude. I appreciate the fact that you didn't come in here disrespecting everybody, trying to make it sound like you know better than we do." And he said, "The way you voiced your opinion really impressed me. Thank you."

I think the man was sincere, but after we had finished our debate I was grateful to hear those words. Lest you think that's a typical comment from their side, you should know that they don't hesitate to attack those with whom they disagree. They'll come after you. But I think this is one of the main reasons they were so upset with Cosby: not just what he said, but how he said it, as well as the fact that he had said it in a very confrontational manner at a meeting of the NAACP.

The gist of the reception of what Cosby had to say went as follows:

- When we needed you back during the civil rights era, you wouldn't say anything.
- We know your private life is in shambles.
- It sounds like you're putting us down, and some on this panel have carried the water for our people in the heat of the day while you were out there getting rich and famous.

It is a classic example of the people rejecting the message because of the messenger.

There's a way these arguments could impact our community. Michael Eric Dyson, who is a scholar, provocative writer, and speaker specializing in black culture, wrote a book called *Is Bill Cosby Right?* In it, he was basically asking what Cosby was trying to accomplish: was he out of his mind, or did he have a valid point? In a sense, he was also challenging the black middle class to remember where they came from. Some have called Dyson the next generation's Cornel West. He's often invited to speak about racial issues, and he felt that Cosby's tone was wrong.[13]

There's no question that our people can do better with regard to personal responsibility and the cross-generational transfer of values. But the question remains, if the family is broken, how do you pass on good values? If Mom is there trying to carry on by herself, there aren't going to be too many Huxtable moments. Sometimes when I speak about these issues, I use the title, "The Huxtables Don't Live Here Anymore."

The Huxtable view of family is a tremendous goal, and I suspect there aren't too many black families who don't watch that show longingly, wishing that it could be that way for them. But it's so far out of focus for most black folks. Even those in the black middle class or on the borderline still have to deal with the problems of single parenting and raising a family in a fast-paced secular culture.

We have to deal with the reality that the stereotypical black neighborhood isn't a safe place to go. Most people, black and white, are intimidated to walk in those parts of town. But that raises another important question: If the black church is, hands down, the most important and most powerful influence in the black neighborhood, how can the neighborhood be in shambles? Where is the moral force of the church? Where is the impact of our Christian faith? And why isn't this quintessential institution of African American life making a greater impact on the culture?

TERMS OF ENGAGEMENT

The black church is starting to turn things around. Our organization, the High Impact Leadership Coalition, is making inroads into some of these areas through community development programs. The book I wrote with George Barna, *High-Impact African-American Churches*, examined some of these things, and we found that the community development aspects of the black church were awesome. But they need to be enhanced and expanded.

The major failing of the black church is not being engaged in more corporate community outreach. I think it is doing well in microfinancing, and it is doing well in having after-school programs and places for kids to have recreational opportunities. But the fundamental building block of every society is the family and the home, and the black church has not done well in getting people to reglue their families or in enforcing biblical moral standards in the home. If we could do those two things, we could greatly reduce the number of out-of-wedlock births and help to stimulate a new era of accountability.

These problems are cultural, but there is a spiritual component. African Americans read the Bible more than any other ethnic group. We pray more and attend church more than whites or Hispanics, and we even fast more. But there is a breakdown between what our people know in their hearts and how it is lived out day to day in the context of the home. It is a form of compartmentalization, by which these individuals are able to separate the kind of biblical morality they practice on Sunday from the demands of personal morality in the home, and that's a problem.

It comes back to the issues of righteousness and justice that I discussed earlier. Although evangelicals have emphasized personal righteousness, it does not necessarily mean they are all living right. There have been many widely publicized examples of evangelical leaders who have fallen from grace. We have a strong spiritual heritage, but I think there is a lot less emphasis on personal holiness and personal responsibility today, and that inevitably leads to more serious problems. I don't mean to be overly judgmental, but when we see statistics like those cited at the beginning of this chapter on family breakdown, single parenting, and out-of-wedlock births, it becomes apparent that we have not done a very good job. Something dramatic is needed, and I strongly believe it needs to be a work of God.

I have preached a series at our church called "Emergency Marriage Help" dealing with the importance of good parenting skills. Midweek we programmed a series of skills-based sessions with role-playing, dramas, and interaction around critical needs like how to communicate more effectively with children and spouses. This was a great program because it dealt with real problems in a straightforward and realistic manner. If we don't train people in basic family skills, they won't be able to change. They will be frustrated, and eventually they will simply stop trying.

The problem of family breakdown is multigenerational, and so many of our young people have never seen an intact family. The closest approximation is what they see on TV. But, as I have said, the Huxtable family is a step beyond what most folks can imagine. There are some other situational comedies that deal with black family life, including shows like *Everybody Hates Chris*, which features a man from our church. The actor Terry Crews is a former player for the Washington Redskins, and he plays the father. But television is not life, and our kids can learn as much bad as good from what they see on TV.

A NEW VISION OF SOCIETY

Eventually, it comes back to training and empowering the family to take care of itself. And that may also mean encouraging aunts and uncles to help look after their nephews and nieces. But how do we prepare mothers, fathers, and these other relatives to compete with all the influences coming from outside the home? There are a lot of people targeting black kids through their music, movies, and fashions. Kids tend to be more affluent these days, and they sometimes spend shocking amounts of money on these things, and a lot of it is harmful.

Young people are saturated with rap music and a kind of entertainment that is little short of pornography. The morals are bad, and the messages are disturbing. Obviously, there is a spiritual battle going on in the culture, and it is almost impossible to counter all the negative influences on our children. Kids are naturally rebellious in the first place, and many times they will put on one face for their parents and another for their friends.

There is another problem that is not quite so obvious. Since kindergarten, our kids have been indoctrinated with the idea that they are special. Teachers tell them, "It's all about you!" And some of us remember when Jesse Jackson was leading crowds of young black kids in the chant, "I am somebody!" With so much history, it is hardly surprising to see new research showing that today's young people are the most narcissistic generation in history.

In 2007, Sarah Konrath at the University of Michigan analyzed the responses of 16,475 college students nationwide who had taken the Narcissistic Personality Inventory survey between 1982 and 2006. Their conclusion, presented in the report "Egos Inflating Over Time," was that young people today are the most self-absorbed and self-centered generation they have ever seen since scientists first began studying the subject.[14]

One thing we can do in terms of getting the younger generation to be less self-centered and to care about other people is to appeal to their desire to get involved in a hands-on manner. I believe most kids want to make a difference. They want their lives to matter, but there has to be a greater sense of personal involvement. Let me give you an example.

All through her college years, my oldest daughter, Joni Michele, was a volunteer with Habitat for Humanity. During her undergraduate work at Williams College in Massachusetts, she was able to go along on Saturdays, in the midst of what was arguably one of the heaviest workloads of any college in America, and to make time to help these folks build houses for disadvantaged families.

She did that because she had a heart to get involved and make a difference in the world.

She was helping to change things, but over time I could see that there were changes in her as well. Helping others made a difference in her worldview. I think this is something the black community needs to begin to do. Some in the black community always seem to be asking what others can do for them, but I would suggest it is time for African Americans to get involved in helping others. We all need to pitch in and help those who are less fortunate.

Serving other people when there is nothing in it for you is a transforming process. We can have all sorts of food pantries and soup kitchens to help those in need, but if it is only the older people who do it, then all the valuable lessons that come from serving others unselfishly will be lost on the young. They truly need this sort of experience to help them become more mature.

Helping others provides a double blessing: you are providing a blessing for them, but giving unselfishly blesses you in return. I remember hearing someone say that he almost felt guilty for the time he spent doing volunteer work because he felt so good afterward. But there is no reason to feel guilty about helping someone else, because the blessing is designed into it. I believe that is the way God meant for it to be. When personal involvement and tangible results come together, that can be a transforming experience.

If we could just get that message out there—to care as much about the well-being of others as we care about ourselves—it would transform the world. This is why the biblical commandment to love the Lord and to love your neighbor as you love yourself is so important. If we only care about ourselves and our own family, we are at least partly responsible for the bitterness that exists in this society. Just think what it would be like if every one of us would make the effort to find one project, one person, or one charitable cause where we could pitch in and make a difference. When we begin to care for others, we are suddenly a part of making the world a better place to live.

Working for Justice

Dr. King was such an extraordinary leader for all of us because of the "I have a dream!" declaration. But in order for that dream to really work and change the way we live, there is going to have to be some kind of greater vision of what we want the world to look like that we can all buy into. The Bible says, "Where there is no vision, the people perish" (Prov. 29:18). If our worldview stops at the end of our noses, then we will always be frustrated and angry whenever we are challenged to see beyond our own wants and interests. But when people have an image in their minds of the way things ought to be, they will start seeing their dreams fulfilled. When they understand their responsibility to other people and to the community, they will spend a lot less time just fighting endless battles on less important fronts.

That is the mature way of seeing our place in society, but to get to that point we will have to overcome a lot of resistance in the community. One of the surprising things that George Barna and I discovered in the research for our book was that black teenagers in particular are very negative about race relations in America. You would think that all the changes in American culture over the last forty years would give them a more positive outlook, but that is not the case.

Forty years ago, blacks were second-class citizens, interracial marriages were a major problem, blacks were seldom able to rise to the top levels in their field, and there were many other barriers to blacks in society. But that has all changed. It is certainly not perfect, but blacks have much greater social mobility today than ever before.

Black families are generally portrayed in a positive light in television sitcoms and the movies, and African Americans are not only among the most popular celebrities and sports heroes but are also heads of giant corporations. We are well represented in the political process at the state, local, and national levels, and an African American is a serious contender in the race for the White House.

So where is the disconnect that causes so many young people to say, "Things are going to be bad for me"?

What it says, in part, is that we still have work to do. And if we don't start shaping the way our young people see their culture, we are going to continue seeing the kinds of racial unrest that we saw in the Jena situation. What we observed in that highly publicized case in Louisiana was a demonstration of the anger that has been transferred to the young people from the previous generation. The hope for a color-blind society that Dr. King spoke about had not been successfully transferred. Instead, there was a lot of unresolved anger.

Instead of compassion, the reports from Jena demonstrated hatred on both sides. As a Christian minister, that is very disturbing to me. The civil rights movement was founded on love. It was nonviolent to the core. Dr. King had his issues, but his message to America was based on the Word of God, and I believe that the civil rights movement under his leadership was a move of God for righteousness and justice.

When it comes down to their understanding of justice, a lot of people in the black community don't really trust the police, the judges, or the justice system. Many blacks feel they have been victimized by the culture. So a better understanding of the relationship between righteousness and justice is essential. Somehow we have to take a second look at these things, and in moral terms, so that change and growth can begin. The first thing we need to do is continue the process of reconciliation between blacks and whites. That is not an easy one, but it is essential. Then we need to help our young people understand that it is not just a matter of us and them; we are all in this thing called civilization together.

CONCRETE EXAMPLES

One way or another, we are going to have to deal with inner-city poverty if we expect to make lasting changes in the African American community. We don't have to get into the dark recesses of black poverty, but we do need to think more creatively about how we are going to deal with these problems. The black churches are doing a lot, as I have said, but there is not much in the way of substantive public policy in this area. There are, however, some interesting models for how constructive change can happen, and one of those is a remarkable story from one of the most impoverished corners of the world.

One of the best examples of innovative community development I have ever come across is the story of a new program of microfinancing developed by the Bangladeshi scholar and banker Muhammad Yunus, who won the Nobel Peace Prize in 2006 for his work in encouraging economic development in the poorest neighborhoods of his home country.

Dr. Yunus launched the Grameen Bank on the idea that people with little or no assets of their own should still be able to invest in small businesses of their own. They can leverage themselves out of poverty by learning how to develop indigenous businesses. In particular, he found that very small loans to individuals engaged in manufacturing furniture and other domestic goods could have a tremendous impact.

In the early twentieth century, blacks in most American cities and towns had few resources to deal with. Those who went into business for themselves generally got money from friends or family members because they weren't able to secure traditional loans from the banks. This is the situation in Bangladesh today, so there is an interesting parallel there that caught my eye.

Dr. Yunus was a well-educated economist who had taught at universities in this country. But when he began considering what he could do to help the people of his home country, he came upon a group of women who made wooden stools. Their work was excellent, and there was a ready market for these stools, but they couldn't afford to buy the raw materials. So Dr. Yunus gave them twenty-seven dollars out of his own pocket, which isn't much by our standards, but it was a great deal of money in that country. And with that modest investment, these women were able to buy the supplies they needed and manufacture and sell their goods.

At the end of the day, the lives of these people were transformed. They were able to buy what they needed, they made the stools and sold them, and for the first time they had a profit that they were able to reinvest in the business. Little by little, they became tremendously successful. That simple act convinced Yunus that this was a fundamental process that could be repeated in many other places. So he began testing his idea in all sorts of areas.

If he could stimulate such a dramatic turnaround with limited funds out of his own pocket, what if he could replicate this process dozens, or hundreds, or even thousands of times? He knew now that his theory could actually work. This convinced him to found the Grameen Bank, which has now funded more than $3.8 billion in loans to approximately 2.8 million individuals and families. That is small money by any kind of American standard, but the payback in terms of community development and poverty relief is absolutely mind-boggling.

RENEWING THE DREAM

I have to believe that Grameen Bank could also be a model for economic development in our own communities. There is a bank in the DC metropolitan area called Collective Banking Group, run by a Harvard MBA, and they pull together churches in our area for community development. They have approximately $130 million in assets, primarily in savings and other investments, and they have been able to fund low-interest loans and mortgages, and it is apparently working. Most importantly, it is not government money.

The easy answer, which the politicians always seem to favor, is to get government involved. But any time the government gets involved, it gets complicated beyond belief and seldom helps those who really need the assistance. How much better to have community-based organizations run by friends and neighbors who understand the need and can provide the options that will actually simplify and improve the situation.

In his book *Banker to the Poor*, Muhammad Yunus describes in detail how the process works. As I was reading his story, I realized that it was out of his heartfelt compassion for these people that he began making the initial investments.[15] When he began, he had to convince the commercial bankers that these artisans were good investments. Small home-based businesses could not begin to offer the kinds of guarantees that would normally be expected for a commercial loan. Their loans could not be collateralized in the normal way, which meant that Dr. Yunus had to do some serious convincing.

Eventually he persuaded the bankers that men and women with tangible skills do have something valuable to offer. They could make furniture that people were willing to buy, and that was the simple beginning. Yunus was not trying to make them into entrepreneurs or corporate officers. He did not need to teach them all the ins and outs of doing business. He was simply working with their natural aptitudes and skills, and along the way helping them to make a profit with what they already knew.

The individual in that situation knows that his skill is his greatest asset, and if someone gives him the opportunity to turn his skill into something greater, he will almost always jump at the chance. He will do everything in his power not to default on that loan, because his livelihood and the well-being of his wife and children depend on it. That is how black businesses first came into being during the Reconstruction Era, and I believe that model is still viable.

Economic reform does not have to be complex; it merely has to serve the needs of the individuals involved. By the same token, I believe social, moral, and cultural reform can happen in much the same way, on the basis of our common interests and needs. The results of the 2004 presidential election proved that the mind-set of African Americans is changing. Although most blacks still voted for John Kerry and the Democrats, black conservatives gave

Bush the cushion he needed to win in Ohio and Florida. Exit polls revealed that a sizeable number of blacks ranked abortion, gay marriage, and school prayer as priority issues, and new multiracial alliances were formed around those issues.

For many African American values voters, black genocide (with over two million black babies aborted in just the last four years) and family disintegration (with nearly 70 percent of all black babies born to unwed mothers) were serious moral problems they could not in good conscience ignore. Those weren't the only problems, of course: black poverty is a major concern, as are education, health care, and prison reform. But a substantial number of African Americans believed their voice mattered at the polls, and that vote of confidence gave the conservative Republican ticket the edge.

Unfortunately, most of our old-school civil rights leaders are still living in the past. Instead of recognizing that the black community is changing and our people are moving on, they are still fighting yesterday's civil rights battles and preaching a doctrine of anger, bitterness, and fear. That wasn't Dr. King's vision, and it certainly wasn't his way. The dream he enunciated from the steps of the Lincoln Memorial was for unity, opportunity, and reconciliation. Meanwhile, the rabble-rousers are making waves over the wrong issues, and in the process making the image of civil rights seem a lot more like civil wrongs.

■ ■ ■ ■

CHAPTER FOUR

A Quiet Revolution

O N FEBRUARY 3, 2005, I WAS ON THE SET OF *THE TAVIS SMILEY Show*. The article about the High Impact Leadership Coalition had appeared on the front page of the *Los Angeles Times* two days before,[1] and apparently a lot of black leaders were afraid a segment of the black community was leaving the "plantation" and throwing their support behind the Republican Party's moral agenda. If that happened, it would mean these so-called "values voters" weren't just a bunch of white guys from the South; they were a racially diverse group of people from all sorts of neighborhoods and backgrounds.

In the months prior to the Bush victory in 2004, I had seen what I believed to be the beginnings of a new partnership between the religious Right and morally conservative African Americans. Reflecting on those views, I had written my editorial in the *New York Sun* a few days before the election, saying, "The new black church is helping the black community rise above the devalued lover syndrome by recommending that she end her longstanding, tawdry affair with the Democratic Party." I went on to say, "An uncompromising generation of black Christians is emerging. These people are bold enough to dream that they can help create a just and moral America."[2]

But as I soon found out, some of our black leaders thought those were fighting words. How could a black pastor possibly suggest that it was time to reconsider our decades-long addiction to the Democratic gravy train? While the language that was used during my interview on BET may not have been quite that incendiary, that is basically what Tavis Smiley wanted to know as well. When we went on camera, Tavis said, "Let me just ask what you think the president's outreach to black America vis-à-vis black churches accomplished in this last election?"[3]

My answer was simple enough. I said, "Well, I think it got him elected." But Tavis wasn't buying it. He pointed out that there was only a 9 to 11 percent shift of black voters toward the GOP in the election, and he said, "But you argue that got him elected?"

"Well, think about it," I said. "Only sixty thousand votes made the difference in Ohio....If Bush lost Ohio, he lost the race. So, really, they doubled the vote in Ohio, and that made the difference. In Florida, there also was a doubling of the black vote, but in those swing states, there was a major difference, and black Christians voted just like the normative mainstream Christian community. But we didn't get anything in return. We only got the privilege of saying, 'Hey, some of the things we were afraid of may not be acted out.' But that's not a positive movement. That's just protecting territory, and I believe we need to advance the cause of Christians. But more specifically, black America needs to be taken seriously."

After the broadcast, Tavis told me he had always wanted to produce a political document like *The Black Contract With America on Moral Values* that we had published the previous month and that we had just been discussing on his program. If he did it, he said, his agenda would be somewhat broader and more secular.

STANDING OUR GROUND

To my surprise, a few days later I was invited to take part in the 2005 Black State of the Union event hosted by Tavis Smiley on the PBS Television Network. The title he used for that forum was "The Black Contract With America." However, a few weeks after the event, he changed the name to "The Covenant With Black

America," and that was the title of the *New York Times* best-selling book he published in 2006.[4]

As I have argued from the start, the idea that black voters may need to rethink their politics (and take another look at the covenants they have made with the liberal establishment) is an idea whose time has come. Smiley is a liberal—there is no doubt about that—and I am an evangelical conservative. But we both agree that African American voters are an important constituency, and those who are seeking our votes need to take our interests seriously. Tavis and I also agree that blacks should not vote strictly on party lines, but there are many issues on which we part ways.

When I accepted the invitation to participate in the Black State of the Union, I knew I would be virtually alone in defending the conservative agenda. As it turned out, there was one other conservative in the group, but that didn't make my job any easier. Many speakers took potshots at what I had to say, and the studio audience was loudly supportive of those who advanced some of the most radical views. I am sorry to say, some of the loudest cheering seemed to be for Minister Farrakhan, whose comments were, frankly, outrageous.

Nevertheless, I went into it knowing I would be in the minority, because I had an agenda too. I wanted to be sure that, at the very least, the men and women who attended that event, or who watched it on television, would hear from someone who was willing to stand his ground and defend the Christian point of view. Unfortunately, when Tavis Smiley invited the Republican candidates in the 2008 presidential campaign to participate in a debate on PBS, the frontrunners were not willing to attend.

Rudy Giuliani, John McCain, Mitt Romney, and Fred Thompson all declined the invitation, while the six second-tier candidates accepted. Senator Sam Brownback; former Arkansas Governor Mike Huckabee; and Representatives Duncan Hunter of California, Ron Paul of Texas, and Tom Tancredo of Colorado all accepted the invitation, as did conservative activist and former UN Ambassador Alan Keyes. But much the same thing had happened the previous summer when all but one of the GOP contenders declined to participate in a debate on the Spanish language network Univision. Only Duncan Hunter attended.

Of course, it is not hard to understand why the candidates declined. They didn't want to participate, as some of them admitted, because they knew they would be in hostile territory. The questions would probably be slanted to make them look bad, and the audience would be against them regardless what they said. As one candidate put it, "Why should I give the Democratic Party sound bites they can use against me in their TV ads?"

There may be some logic in this argument, but it did not play well with the minority community. By distancing themselves from that audience, the leading Republican candidates played into the hands of their opponents, who immediately accused them of prejudice and disrespect for black voters. In an interview with *USA Today*, Tavis Smiley lambasted the frontrunners: "No one should be elected president of this country in 2008 if they think that along the way they can ignore people of color. If you want to be president of all America, you need to speak to all Americans."[5] By refusing to take the heat, the candidates managed to give their critics exactly what they were looking for: an opportunity to label them as cowards and racists.

A TIME FOR CHANGE

The Democrats were not the only ones who felt that snubbing the PBS debates was a mistake. Frank Luntz, a leading Republican pollster, told MSNBC that rejecting Smiley's invitation "undermined much of the progress George W. Bush had made in attracting minority voters in the 2000 and 2004 presidential elections. Hispanics and African-Americans," he said, "account for about a fifth of the electorate." And that is too big and too important a constituency for the candidates to ignore.[6]

Because of the nature of the debates, I thought I ought to be there, so I drove up to the campus of Morgan State University in

Baltimore to see what happened. As I sat in the audience, I couldn't help but notice that at least 40 percent of the attendees were white. The questions they were asked were well reasoned and professionally delivered. I also observed that some of the biggest applause lines went to Tom Tancredo, Ron Paul, and Ambassador Keyes, even though their views on most things weren't those of the stereotypical black voter.

Real change always requires risk and rethinking old habits. To get people to the point where they are willing to listen to our arguments and consider new and better options, sometimes we have to go into hostile territory. Even if his motives were different from my own, I believe Tavis Smiley was right about his assessment of the candidates' lack of attendance.

In February 2006, I was invited for the second time to take part in a nationally televised discussion with ten religious and civil rights leaders at the New Birth Missionary Baptist Church in suburban Atlanta. Among the participants this time were Jesse Jackson; Al Sharpton; Cornel West; Harry Belafonte; Melvin Watt, who is chairman of the Congressional Black Caucus; Representatives John Conyers of Michigan and Sheila Jackson Lee of Texas; as well as civil rights leader Wade Henderson, Minister Louis Farrakhan, and Senator Jackie Winters of Oregon; along with myself and Bishop Eddie Long, in whose church the seminar took place.

It was a who's who of black leaders, primarily from the far Left of the political spectrum, brought together by Tavis Smiley and PBS Television to talk about the state of the union for African Americans. This was the second meeting of this kind, coming shortly after the nationally televised State of the Union Address by President Bush. It was clearly meant to be a slap in the face to the president and the policies of the GOP, while issuing a battle cry to the African American community to reignite the dying embers of the civil rights movement.

For weeks after that event, people in our community talked about it so much I had to ask myself, "Why do our people even want to talk about social problems and race issues in America anymore?" Shouldn't we be more disgusted with the unaccountable leaders in Washington, the bandits in our neighborhoods, and the attitude of defeatism that has kept so many of our people in a kind of self-imposed bondage? Aren't we fed up with all the endless rhetoric and moral hypocrisy of these race hustlers?

As I indicated in the previous chapter, the average black American believes that fundamental changes are necessary, but most do not think we need to make wholesale changes or start over again to get on the right track. We believe America can be a great nation by making a few minor adjustments. So we listen to what various people are saying, discuss our problems, pray for the kinds of change that will help us move in a new direction, and then take our beliefs and our political convictions into the voting booth.

After the PBS broadcast, I was in contact with Christian leaders all over the country, both black and white. I said I was convinced we can achieve common ground with white and Hispanic voters in order to solve many of the nation's most pressing problems, and I listened to what these men and women had to say. My approach is a blend of conservative thinking and common sense; there is nothing mysterious about it. It is simply a matter of recognizing the areas where change is needed and then working together to find the simplest and most practical solutions.

I believe the time is ripe for major changes in the way black America thinks about our problems. We don't need loud, angry race-hustlers cluttering the airwaves with their charges of institutional racism. We need leaders with level heads who can bring about constructive change by sound judgment and diplomatic interaction with others. If the conservative movement can attract strong, visionary leaders with genuine courage and a measure of personal appeal, I think we can make a real difference. Are there values-centered leaders out there that we can support? I believe there are. Are there issues where change is needed that blacks and whites can agree on? Of course there are, and we need to start building bridges now in order to begin that process.

The title of a new book by Alan Deutschman says it very well, *Change or Die*. As I have said repeatedly in these pages, the change we need means tearing down some old walls, making some new friends, creating some new alliances, and trying some new approaches to achieve the goals that all of us have for our families, our communities, and our nation. But equally important, it may also mean that we need to make some changes in ourselves and reconsider some of our old habits in order to get to where we want to go.

NEW TACTICS FOR A NEW ERA

We cannot hope to achieve our dreams if there is warfare within our own ranks. "A house divided against itself will not stand" (Matt. 12:25). We don't need to be fighting with each other, but we cannot keep fighting "the man" as if it were still 1965 and the blood's still red on the Pettis Bridge. This is a new century and a new era, and we are going to need new methods of doing things. I believe we have a unique opportunity at this moment to change the world, but not in the old ways—not by violence and rage, but by a serious, Christ-centered appeal to reason through reconciliation, diplomacy, disciplined prayer, and purposeful political engagement.

For more than thirty years, many of our black leaders worked tirelessly to mobilize their followers through confrontational political action. They used the broadcast media and massive public demonstrations to try to change the way Americans think about race. That strategy led to a number of changes in our laws and the creation of many controversial new policies that made race a front-burner issue. But did it make things better, or did it merely make things different? There is just as much resentment and suspicion today as there ever was, if not more. And while a lot of African Americans have made a better life for themselves, it has been primarily through education and hard work. Meanwhile, many of our black neighborhoods are still in chaos.

Over the last eight years, conservative Christians have made great strides in the culture by expressing their religious beliefs at the polls. In each of the last two national elections, 2004 and 2006, nearly 60 million evangelical voters turned out to make a difference at the ballot box. They focused on a handful of priorities that pressed the cultural envelope of both thought and communication. To call their efforts successful would be an understatement. They have begun a quiet revolution that, I believe, may well transform the world as we know it.

They haven't done it by riots and rallies but by taking advantage of the sophisticated communications media at their disposal, including radio, television, the Internet, phone banks, mass mailings, the development of targeted surveys and get-out-the-vote campaigns, and a thousand other ways. The heart of that message is still the Christian gospel and an appeal to what sociologist James Q. Wilson has called "the moral sense." Yes, it is socially and politically motivated, but at bottom the appeal of the evangelical message is to love the Lord your God with all your heart, soul, mind, and strength, and to love your neighbor as yourself (Luke 10:27). It is the great commandment, and it is perhaps the hardest challenge we will ever have.

The evangelical game plan involves setting priorities and building coalitions of like-minded individuals in all segments of society. It means holding our own gains in Congress while appealing to Democrats who share our convictions on social and moral issues. In addition to the cultivation of new candidates and building the base of potential new voters, the media engine of the evangelical movement is focusing more and more on reaching out to new communities.

One of the most promising of these is the appeal to young adults in the Gen-X and Gen-Y age groups who are disenchanted with the immorality, self-centeredness, and materialism of the previous generation. These young people are more socially aware than their predecessors, and their interests are generally motivated by their Christian faith and genuine compassion for others. The outreach to the boomer generation is still strong, but as the evangelical outreach continues to expand to new groups and new categories of "values voters," I'm convinced that the elections of 2008, 2010, and 2012 will be decided by the most diverse group of voters in our history.

There will be efforts to divide and block that agenda, of course. There are liberal groups that consider politically active evangelical voters to be the single greatest threat to their own success, and they will do anything in their power to prevent an evangelical resurgence. Liberal Christians have been trying to break the unity of evangelicals for years by sponsoring antiwar rallies, environmentalist crusades, "commitment services" for homosexual couples, and other such events, while loudly proclaiming their moral superiority on these issues. They would like us to believe that the American people have already given up on the goals and values of the "religious Right." But most of that is spin and wishful thinking. The liberal church remains a tiny percentage of the Christian church today.

DIVIDING THE BASE

A good example of the way the liberal media and liberal Christians have tried to slant the news away from what is actually happening can be seen in a major story headlined, "Emphasis Shifts for New Breed of Evangelicals," that was published on the front page of the *New York Times* on May 21, 2007.[7] In the first paragraph, the writers of the article credit the evangelical Christian movement with shaping the political landscape in this country since the 1980s. But they are quick to say that the agenda is now shifting and "exposing new fissures" that could mean the death of the conservative Christian movement as we know it.

The passing of Rev. Jerry Falwell one week earlier on May 15, 2007, at age seventy-three was emblematic, they say, of the death of the religious Right. They go on to say that "many of the movement's fiery old guard who helped lead conservative Christians into the embrace of the Republican Party are aging and slowly receding from the scene." Taking their place will be a new generation of leaders who shun partisan politics in favor of liberal causes such as AIDS, Darfur, poverty, and global warming. Abortion and same-sex marriage had been emotional issues for their parents' generation, they say, but a new "centrist" position is "evolving" among younger Christians. The issues that motivated older Christians no longer have the same appeal.

While briefly mentioning the work of Falwell, Robertson, Dobson, Charles Colson, and other leaders of the last wave of evangelicals, the writers focus on pastors Rick Warren and Bill Hybels, leaders of two of the largest megachurch congregations in the country. Warren has used profits from his best-selling book *The Purpose-Driven Life* to help eradicate AIDS in Africa. Warren and Hybels, we are told, have also joined with liberal leaders such as Jim Wallis of Sojourners and Ronald Sider of Evangelicals for Social Action in calling for action on global climate change and other "progressive" issues.

Subdividing evangelicals into conservative, centrist, and modernist camps seems to be one of the objectives of the liberal media. Citing a number of polls that show evangelicals to be more conservative than the general public on issues such as immigration and the environment, the *Times* article suggests there are "tremors of change" within the Christian community, and that liberal Christians such as Democratic candidate Barack Obama have given a new legitimacy to the practice of speaking about one's faith on the campaign trail. In other words, talking about faith is all right so long as it is "progressive" or "modernist" faith, and safely "nontraditional."

This article offers several examples of Christians who have seen the light and moved away from their conservative roots toward a more "enlightened" and less politically engaged way of thinking. A thirty-two-year-old graduate of Jerry Falwell's Liberty University who traded politics for an interest in "media and the arts" is quoted as saying, "I believe politics just isn't as important to younger evangelicals as it has been for the older generation because we recognize from experience that politics does not shape the morality of a culture. It simply reflects what the larger culture wants."

One wonders what "experience" the young man might have that warrants such a claim. Politics happens to be the means by which we elect those who will determine public policy and make the laws that help to "shape the morality of a culture." In democratic societies, "what the larger culture wants" is generally a consensus issue, which is normally decided by political choices and each citizen's right to vote. We call that "majority rule." It is one of the most foundational principles of our republican form of government. But articles of this type are not written to inform or encourage, but to shape the public's attitudes about the Christian Right.

An Irresistible Force

During the long campaign season, many positions on critical issues will be put forth by candidates who are Left, Right, and center. Evangelicals will continue to focus on the sanctity of life at birth and in the laboratory, the importance of the family and traditional marriage, and protecting our borders and the historical values and traditions of the American people. On the other hand, the Christian Left will continue to advocate "progressive" ideas that are meant to soften and water down all those issues. The goal of the Left is to raise questions in the minds of the faithful, while challenging the historic beliefs of the Moral Majority.

Liberal periodicals have had a field day in recent months with revelations of immorality among some of the leaders of the evangelical movement, whether it is allegations of corruption in Congress; the widely publicized report that Senator Larry Craig of Idaho was arrested for soliciting a homosexual encounter with a plainclothes policeman in the Minneapolis airport; the revelation that the president of the National Association of Evangelicals, Ted Haggard, may have done something similar; or the long-running scandals involving so-called "pedophile priests."

Meanwhile, the religious Left have become the lapdogs of the Democratic Party. Social and religious liberals such as Jim Wallis and Ronald Sider, mentioned above, appear more like the public relations agency for the Democratic National Committee. While conservatives call for greater personal responsibility and accountability in dealing with critical social concerns, for liberals it always comes down to a problem that can only be solved by more government spending.

Family breakdown, out-of-wedlock childbirth, law and order issues, and community renewal were all moral and religious problems long before they became political concerns. It is true that individual involvement and works of charity and compassion are essential in dealing with all these matters, but the most effective way of dealing with these problems is by mobilizing an energized community of concerned citizens who are motivated by their religious convictions. That is the environment in which compassion is transformed into constructive change.

Regardless of how hard they may try to change the subject or shift the focus, the religious Left is still just as feckless and ineffective as they have always been. They lack genuine moral heft and have little to offer but the weak soup of compromise. Meanwhile, the conservative evangelical community has delivered more than sixty million voters to the polls in past elections. There have always been and will always be differences of opinion within our ranks, just as there are differences of affluence and ethnicity. But the conservative Christian community, made up of men and women from all walks of life, will continue to be the dominant force in the political process for years to come.

Men and women in the evangelical movement will be watching carefully during the various stages of the presidential race as the candidates discuss and debate the issues. In time, the candidates will reveal their core values, character, and their positions on the issues we care about. At that point, the Christian community will begin to move together as an irresistible force, until they have lifted one deserving candidate into the winner's circle.

In some cases we may have to hold our noses while we vote, choosing the lesser of two evils. But even so, one thing ought to be perfectly clear: the nation hasn't seen the last of the evangelical movement by a long shot. Like Joshua at the gates of Jericho, we are ready, armed, and dressed for battle. As many of our fathers and grandfathers who served in the Second World War would have said, we are in it for the duration.

REVOLUTIONARY LANGUAGE

Over the last several years, I have occasionally heard Democratic politicians using the term "the third way" in conversations about politics. Instead of talking about issues as either conservative or liberal, they are saying we need a third way that is a compromise between the extremes. On the surface, it sounds like they are talking about the middle ground between Left and Right. However, it turns out to be a lot more than that.

Some readers will remember Hillary Clinton's former adviser, Michael Lerner, who once claimed that "the third way" would become the new way of governing in America. I have not heard the term much since then, and I suspect that is because most intelligent folks quickly realized that this was really just a clever turn of phrase meant to persuade the masses that "our way is the right way, and everybody else is wrong."

As I have thought about everything that is happening today in the political revolution that is taking place in this country, I have been impressed by the energy and resourcefulness of Christian conservatives. They take a lot of abuse but keep on coming—I like that. But I have encountered a lot of frauds and fakes along the way, posing as viable solutions to America's problems. Some of these ideas are naïve or superficial, but others are truly dangerous; and I have to agree with conservative activist David Horowitz that attempts by liberals to pass off a political "third way" as a legitimate option may be one of the most deceptive and dangerous ideas.

In a lengthy treatise published on the Jewish World Review Web site, Horowitz writes that "the third way" is actually "a term from the lexicon of the far Left with a long and dishonorable pedigree...." In the 1930s, Nazis used the term to characterize their own brand of national socialism as the middle way between the socialism of the Soviet Union and the capitalism of the West. Trotskyites then used it to distinguish between their kind of Marxism and the Stalinist variety. In the 1960s, the so-called "New Left" used this term to define their kind of Marxist social revolution as the midpoint between Soviet-style socialism and American-style democracy.[8]

But as the sordid history of each of these failed ideologies should tell us, there is no third way. There is, as Horowitz writes insightfully, only "the capitalist, democratic way based on private property and individual rights—a way that leads to liberty and universal opportunity. And there is the socialist way of group identities, group rights, a relentless expansion of the political state, restricted liberty and diminished opportunity." The third way is not a path to the future. Rather, it is an attempt by those who believe in growing the size of the "nanny state" and submerging our individual rights to convince gullible people that their ideas might actually work.

But their ideas never work, and to the degree that politicians, pundits, and the mainstream media continue to promote large social programs and left-wing policies "for our own good," they are doing all Americans a terrible disservice. When we think about what is really at stake in the battles taking place between the Left and the Right in this country—particularly in the coming elections—it is vital that we think about the risks we will face if we buy into the illusion that a bigger and more powerful central government is the answer to our problems.

THE FROG IN THE KETTLE

One of the most memorable images that comes to mind is the title of an excellent book, written by my former coauthor and friend George Barna, *The Frog in the Kettle.*[9] The metaphor George used in the title of that book is of a frog in a large kettle of water sitting on the stove. Turn the heat up slowly enough and the frog will never realize what is happening to him until it is too late and he is cooked. For generations, many Americans—and I would have to emphasize especially many African Americans—have been persuaded that their interests are best served by a bigger, more powerful government with unlimited resources. Even our own black leaders have told us that government can bring peace and harmony and help us accomplish all our noble goals.

That notion is false. Large and unrestricted governments are among the greatest evils mankind has ever faced on this earth, which is why the Founding Fathers of the American republic fought so hard to give us a limited government, a republican legislative process, and a legacy of individual liberty and personal accountability. If big government were the answer, they could have remained under the thumb of European monarchs, but the colonists risked their lives to escape from the tyranny of the imperial state. Then they fought for eight long years to establish our freedoms on this continent, so that future generations of Americans could live by the grace of God according to their own covenants and honest labors.

I am not saying that everything is perfect—far from it. But when it comes to race relations and the social and political divisions that remain between black and white Americans, we do not need government-mandated solutions and "third way" compromises. What we need is to work for reconciliation and understanding by coming together in ways that will allow us to discuss our differences and concerns openly and without prejudice. Then, like the free people we are, we can decide which things we can live with and which we can't.

There are all kinds of conservatives—fiscal conservatives, sometimes called new conservatives or "neocons"; social conservatives, which some journalists refer to as "so-cons"; and traditional Christian conservatives, referred to as the "religious Right." There are also some who identify themselves as moderate conservatives.

But in the face of the challenges we face from the Left—from political liberals and moderates as well as the occasional "third way" liberals—we cannot afford to let the labels and minor distinctions distract us from the main things that bind us together.

Unless we want to settle back into the kettle while the heat is rising and the water is beginning to boil all around us, we need to think seriously about what it is we truly believe in. Most of us would say that freedom is essential. I would add that righteousness and justice are equally important. Our Christian faith demands that we look beyond past hurts and resentment and find new ways to work together in order to preserve the values we hold dear. That, I believe, is the foundation of a new paradigm and a model for a political realignment that can transform our world. But, more importantly, it is the biblical paradigm for a dynamic faith that calls all God's children to live and work together in one accord for the common good.

REJECTING A FAILED LEGACY

The brilliant black economist and social philosopher Thomas Sowell has written many inspirational works from a politically conservative perspective on the problems with modern liberalism. In one recent article, he argues that the most common element of liberal social policy is the Left's veneration of failure.[10] At first that does not make much sense: is he saying that a vast segment of the public, and liberal policymakers in Washington worship the idea of failure?

Well, yes. That is what he is saying. The reason is because liberals are addicted to big government, big expensive tax-and-spend programs, and more and more armies of liberal bureaucrats to run the welfare state. Sowell writes, "Progress in general seems to hold little interest for people who call themselves 'progressives.' What arouses them are denunciations of social failures and accusations of wrongdoing."[11]

Evangelical Christians believe that men and women are predisposed to sin by what the Bible calls our "sin nature." In general, liberals don't buy into the idea of "sin." They believe there are only misjudgments and mistakes that can be corrected by better laws and more regulations. For the Left, failure is what motivates them. As Sowell observes sardonically, despite what the Left may say about their compassion for the poor, the poor are merely a convenient weapon for denouncing the meanness and corruption of capitalist societies.

If the poor ever stopped being poor, Sowell writes, they would no longer merit the attention of the Left. If they should discover that changes in the economy or some other type of innovative solution has led to dramatic reductions in poverty, little notice would be taken, and even less celebration. When Karl Marx delivered his manifesto for the impoverished working classes of Europe, his aim wasn't to improve the lot of the poor but to attack and destroy capitalism. In fact, says Sowell, he was disappointed and angry when the workers began earning better pay and lost their revolutionary zeal. He goes on to say:

> At one point, Marx wrote to his disciples, "The working class is revolutionary or it is nothing." Think about that. Millions of human beings mattered to him only in so far as they could serve as cannon fodder in his jihad against the existing society. If they refused to be pawns in his ideological game, then they were "nothing."[12]

But then, even more powerfully, Sowell writes that, "Blacks are to the Left today what the working class were to Marx in the 19th century—pawns in an ideological game. Blacks who rise out of poverty are of no great interest to the Left, unless the way they do so is by attacking society. The poverty rate among black married couples has been in single digits since 1994, but the Left has shown no more interest in why that is so than they have shown in why many millions of people have risen out of poverty in Latin America or in China and India."[13]

Over the years, the Left has convinced millions of Americans that the social advances made by minorities and women in this century are the result of the liberal movements of the 1960s. But their claims are baseless, since most of the real gains in these areas were achieved prior to the sixties. Furthermore, the countless failures endured by society in the wake of that revolutionary era—including runaway crime rates, sexual profligacy, the disintegration of black families, and ghetto riots that have left many black communities destitute after more than forty years—are conveniently ignored by the revisionists. Whatever does not serve the political ambitions of the Left, as Marx expressed it, is "nothing."

ISSUES WORTH DEFENDING

As we enter into another election season, the rhetoric from both sides has intensified and the volume of the debates has grown increasingly louder. The "miniwars" we call political campaigns are strategically managed, media driven, and extremely well financed. As the political stakes have risen to enormous proportions, the win-at-all-costs mentality is now the order of the day.

Against a backdrop of scandals, accusations, and endless controversy, it would be futile to ignore the public's dissatisfaction with the way business is done in the nation's capital by both of the major political parties. Yet, the media offer a constant barrage of polls and surveys that tell us that America is fed up with the Republican leadership, and Democratic challengers are just waiting to take over the reins of power. At the same time, we hear that minority voters are ready to "throw the bums out." The common theme of many editorials seems to be, "Why vote? The evangelical movement is dead, conservatives are deserting the Republican Party faster than rats leaving a sinking ship, and your votes can't possibly make a difference anyway."

As I have emphasized throughout these pages, I am not buying the Left's spin anymore. I have changed my political leanings, and I believe the conservative Christian community can make a real and lasting difference. Furthermore, I believe it would be immoral to abandon the fight when there are so many issues worth defending. For that reason, I want to touch at this point on eight national issues that are begging for clear leadership from those who are running for office and asking for our votes. There are many things that could be said, but these are some of the questions that will demand answers:

1. The war

The war in the Middle East will likely be one of the primary concerns of voters in the next election. The liberal media have tried to equate the fascist zeal of radical Islam with evangelical fundamentalism, but that is a false analogy. There is a hot war on the ground in Iraq and Afghanistan with those who prefer to convert infidels with the sword. Christian doctrine never condones violence, and we do not believe in conversion by force. As the apostle Paul says, "We do not wrestle against flesh and blood, but against principalities, against powers, against the rulers of the darkness of this age..." (Eph. 6:12).

Our warfare as believers is not with men but with our own sin nature. However, the hot war our young men and women are fighting in the Middle East is to defend our freedoms and to preserve Western society from those who would, in the name of their religion, take away our freedom of conscience and subject us to a hideous ideology. The best response for evangelical leaders in this environment is to speak with compassion about what is truly at stake on the battlefield and what our best and most appropriate response as a nation ought to be.[14]

2. Terrorism

The tenets of radical Islam must be explained to the American people. For the most part, the mainstream media have avoided getting into the details, either out of some misplaced notion of multiculturalism or their desire to posit a false equivalence between all religions. But when we understand what it is the jihadists and terrorists are intent on doing to us, the American people will rally together to protect our nation. I believe they will do so without falling into a xenophobic hatefest if they understand the nature and determination of the enemy. It is not about oil or gold or any other of the commonly used canards we hear from the Left. It is about the survival of our way of life and the future of our children.

3. International relief efforts

Evangelicals have a deep belief in the need for world missions and outreach to the poor and disadvantaged of the world. For centuries it has been Christians who have established hospitals, mercy missions, and sanctuaries for the weak and wounded. The Christian community is by far the most philanthropic institution in Western society, and we are the best equipped to understand not only why it's important to invest in relief effort for hurting peoples, but also to share a message of hope and redemption in the midst of suffering and trauma.

4. Immigration

Immigration has become one of the most pernicious and controversial issues of our day. Illegal immigration is a serious threat to America for many reasons: border security, the rule of law, and the ability to trust our elected officials to protect us from an alien onslaught, just for starters. The idea that the political party who panders most to people who have broken our laws and entered the country illegally will reap a dividend at the polls is shallow and disingenuous thinking.

The frustrations of the American people have never been greater than now, and they will not hesitate to make their feelings known at the polls if our political leaders don't get the picture very soon. It is time for politicians with maturity and moral courage to get involved in this issue and help the American people resolve this national dilemma. Either we are a nation of laws or we are an undisciplined mob, and if we allow our culture to be overwhelmed and transformed by alien hordes, we will deserve our fate.

5. Rebuilding storm-ravaged cities and towns

A compassionate domestic mission will require that government, churches, and local communities come together to aid the millions of men, women, and children who have been displaced by the disasters on our southern coast. The task will not be easy, and the cost will be high, which means that political pressure may be needed to keep these rebuilding projects before the eyes of the nation. For many African Americans, the Hurricane Katrina disaster has become a symbol of class inequity and racial prejudice. But a unified effort of black, white, and Hispanic evangelicals to restore these communities can send a very different message. Leadership in these areas can provide a wonderful example of what grace, mercy, and compassion can accomplish.

6. Character-based education

America's competitive edge in the new global economy depends on continued improvements in technology, service, and organizational leadership. The soft bigotry of low expectations, along with illiteracy and lack of discipline among America's young people, has spread far beyond the ghetto, and our schools are in utter chaos. Government programs such as No Child Left Behind haven't even begun to scratch the surface, and it is doubtful that the "education establishment" will ever have either the willpower or the capacity to make the kinds of changes that are needed.

Politicians and other community leaders need to get involved in this issue now and demand that an education in the fundamentals, including basic literacy, math, science, American history, and other essential subjects, are the right of every child. These should be front-burner issues for the foreseeable future. We do not need more sociology experiments in the classrooms; we need to get back to the fundamentals in order to give every American child the benefits of "a well-ordered mind."

7. Environmental policy reform

Younger Americans in particular have embraced the view that we are stewards of the earth. Not everything these young people are hearing and thinking today is to be trusted, however, since the Left has dominated public school and university classrooms for so many decades and liberal ideologues are using this issue to, once again, grow the size of government. But an interest in caring for the environment and being more responsible for how we live can be a good thing if conservative and evangelical leaders can provide a better understanding of the true meaning of stewardship and our responsibility to the others with whom we share this planet. There is little doubt that this will remain a battleground area for both Left and Right for some time to come, so clear-headed and responsible thinking is greatly needed.

8. Health-care reform

Since the early 1990s when Hillary Clinton tried to tackle comprehensive health-care reform, there has been increasing debate over what sort of reforms are needed and who should pay for the increasing cost of medical care. Mrs. Clinton's efforts were not successful because the public understood that "socialized medicine" has failed everywhere it has been tried. But the problem has not gone away, and it will be important for the next generation of leaders to bring some order out of the chaos. Thoughtful engagement here can make a real difference, preserving what is good about our current systems while exploring new opportunities. Lowering the cost of medical care through tax incentives or market pressure will help, and providing some sort of safety net for those who are unable to afford private health insurance would be a good place to start.

I believe most people will acknowledge that these are some of the most challenging issues of our day, and each demands discussion in greater detail. Despite the media's claims that the era of the Moral Majority and the Christian Coalition is dead and gone, in these pages I have provided evidence that the conservative

Christian movement is alive and well and moving into a newer and more dynamic stage of development. There are many challenges, like those listed above, where responsible and compassionate leaders can demonstrate the wisdom of our values.

The evangelical movement has not been buried, as the media would have us believe; it's not even losing steam. However, it is going through a major transition today as black, white, and Hispanic conservatives learn how to work with one another to achieve our common goals. What is taking place in our homes, churches, and neighborhoods today is nothing short of revolutionary—it is a quiet revolution that will make our influence greater than ever and insure that the efforts of politically engaged evangelicals will be even more robust and more effective in the years ahead than ever before.

■ ■ ■ ■

What We Really Want

IT IS NO SECRET THAT PRESIDENT GEORGE W. BUSH HAS BEEN less than popular with the general public during his second term in the White House. His poll ratings have been miserable, and the media have given him a beating. A front-page article in the *Wall Street Journal* two days after the 2007 State of the Union address was headlined, "Bush's Conservative Base Frets: Key Issues Are Losing Focus."[1] The story said the president's conservative base was disappointed with what he had to say, and they are concerned that the Bush administration has abandoned its core issues. The article also goes on to say that evangelicals are not the only ones who are concerned.

The *Wall Street Journal*/NBC News poll that accompanied the story showed that most conservatives still agree that the war on terror and the war in Iraq ought to remain priority issues, followed by illegal immigration and the economy. However, when asked which social issues were most disturbing, 55 percent of respondents said "declining moral values," 42 percent said "poor control of illegal immigration," 26 percent said "poor quality of public education," and 18 percent indicated that "American jobs moving overseas" was most disturbing. Health insurance and fuel prices ranked lower in both samplings.

Individuals responding to the poll, which was taken a few days before the State of the Union address, were not just "wild-eyed evangelicals." They were conservative Republicans of all stripes—some concerned primarily with fiscal policy, and others for whom social policy was most important. But one fact stood out: it is apparent from these numbers that the "values voters" of the 2000 and 2004 elections have not gone away. And despite media claims that evangelicals have abandoned the cause, the truth is that the religious Right has become better informed and more outspoken on the issues. But the conservative base no longer feels obliged to follow along quietly with whatever their elected officials tell them.

For a long time, white evangelicals felt as though they had painted themselves into a political corner. They felt like their black evangelical counterparts, who have historically supported Democratic leaders with little to show for it. But both these groups have learned their lesson, so today both blacks and whites are taking a more circumspect look at their options. Beyond the politics involved, we now understand that the nation needs to hear the moral voice of the faith community. That is why we refuse to give up and simply go away.

In a video commentary about the president's speech published on the Internet, my friend Tony Perkins of the Family Research Council called the State of the Union address a "lifeless" speech. It was the first time in his presidency that President Bush would have to address a Democrat-controlled Congress, and he spent roughly half the time defending the war in Iraq and Homeland Security issues. But, as Tony Perkins observed, "that same clear and concise determination to defend the culture of America was missing." He went on to say, "I believe the president failed in challenging the new majority to join him in addressing core family and cultural issues....The president failed to draw a line in the sand on behalf of life."[2]

Tony's remarks went right to the heart of the matter. The motivation for returning to the kind of leadership he described should be strong for this president. Today we are seeing a new alliance of black, white, and Hispanic Christians who have come together to demand responsible change and a restoration of moral values in American culture. These grassroots alliances, built around socially conservative issues, ought to be enough to compel leaders of both major parties to try harder to work together. The process of change might be slow and tedious, but it is worth the effort, and it needs to happen.

It is time for a paradigm shift in Washington. The White House and the evangelical movement need to build bridges and find new ways to achieve our objectives. That is what we expect from our leaders. Unfortunately, we have received mostly mixed messages from the White House ever since the 2004 election. The administration has backed away from its support for a federal marriage amendment. They have spoken out of both sides of their mouth on sanctity-of-life issues and rejected our input on a host of social concerns, which accounts for the dismal approval ratings of the president and Congress.

Despite the claims of the liberal media that faith is finished and the religious Right is yesterday's news, a majority of Americans still identify themselves as Christians, and a majority say they are deeply concerned about the decline of moral values. Poll after poll shows that the American people want leaders who will lead with conviction on the issues that matter most to them. They are not going away. Quite the contrary. There is a powerful new force rising in the land, and the men and women who can translate this explosion of new energy from grassroots, politically active Christian voters into an effective political strategy will reap the rewards.

A Political Nightmare

For months I struggled with my emotions about what was happening in Washington. Every time we would put forth an initiative to support pro-family and pro-life causes, or to limit the erosion of our basic freedoms through "hate crimes" legislation and other left-wing tactics, the White House either backed away from the issues or they simply allowed them to pass into law without comment.

The administration seemed to be oblivious to our concerns about the security of U.S. ports, the border with Mexico, the invasion of illegal immigrants in our cities and towns, the flood of substandard goods from China, and even the importance of pro-life policies affecting abortion, stem cell research, and the like. Perhaps most troubling was the fact that top-level officials seemed to think the conservative Christian base no longer mattered, or that our influence had faded.

In order to address some of these issues, and to let the president and his advisers know how we felt about it, I met with a group of Christian leaders who represented literally millions of conservative voters all across America, and we made an appointment to go to the White House and lay out our concerns.

When we arrived, we learned that the president would not be available due to other pressing commitments, but that Tim Goeglein, deputy director of the White House Office of Public Liaison, would be available to meet with us. We were joined by some of our faithful supporters from Congress and the administration, and the chairman of the Republican National Committee, Ken Mehlman, was there. But they told us that chief presidential adviser Karl Rove was too busy to come physically, but we would be able to speak to him for a few minutes by conference call.

Some of the members of our group had flown in from hundreds of miles away for this meeting. They were men whose ministries represented millions of people of all ages, races, and denominations and included some of the biggest names in the evangelical world. In some cases, the budgets they managed exceeded several million dollars annually, and they could mobilize untold millions of supporters on any given day through the print and broadcast facilities they controlled. Yet the White House decided that having an audience with the president's chief adviser by telephone would be enough.

What happened in that meeting was an assault on the entire Christian movement. This was May of 2006, with an important midterm election coming up in November that would determine the majority in both houses of Congress. At that moment there still was a Republican majority in the House and the Senate, but historically the party in power loses as many as thirty seats in the House and five in the Senate in off-year elections, so there was no reason to be complacent about the importance of the election.

But that was the environment. I was on chemotherapy at the time and struggling with some of the aftereffects of those treatments, which didn't help the way I was feeling about the welcome we received. But once the meeting began, Mr. Rove started talking about how well things had gone for the Republicans in the 2004 elections, and he spoke briefly about the challenges for 2006. It seemed to be a fairly routine pep talk, but that is not why we had come.

After he had given us his spiel, we began telling him that we were concerned about the issue of same-sex marriage, and we needed a federal marriage amendment to make sure that the sanctity of marriage and the family were constitutionally protected. We told him we expected the administration to make this a priority, but we had noticed that they seemed to be backing away from the issue. If the president was backing away from it, even though he had indicated his support in the beginning, we felt that would send all the wrong signals.

A War of Words

At that point, Karl Rove went into a long, drawn-out discussion of the campaign, and he said essentially, "Yeah, you guys did help us, but it wasn't just the moral values thing or the marriage amendment thing that got President Bush reelected. It was a number of things: his stance on the war, his economic policies..." and he listed off all the things he had been working on to attract voters to the party.

When he finished talking, he paused for a moment, and I could not restrain myself any longer. I spoke up and said, "Sir, you don't know me, but my name is Bishop Harry Jackson, and I am senior minister of Hope Christian Center in Beltsville, Maryland. I happen to be a registered Democrat. But I've been working with Republicans and with this group of people because of the moral values I represent. I got tired of being taken advantage of by my party. It started feeling like we were in an adulterous relationship with the Democrats. They would show up and demand what they wanted when they wanted it, on their own terms. But they didn't take me to dinner, they didn't buy me flowers, and there was no romance. It was all about meeting their needs."

I said, "Sir, I believe the way you are now treating the evangelical movement in the Republican Party is exactly what happened to us in the Democratic Party, and I want you to know that I don't like it."

As soon as I said those words, there was an explosion on the other end of the line. Karl Rove lit up like a Roman candle, and his voice literally doubled in volume: "Well, Mr. Jackson!" he snapped at me, and from there he was off to the races. He began reading me chapter and verse and telling me where I was wrong, that his party had not rejected evangelicals, but that all sorts of other things had to be taken into consideration. And furthermore, I was being naïve and unrealistic to think that the GOP had deserted the base.

At that point, one of the best-known evangelical leaders in the country lit up, and what happened next was not pretty. He picked up where I left off and told Karl Rove that the evangelical community has had enough of being patronized and exploited by the GOP, and we were not going to sit around waiting for them to get the message. But it got even worse from there. Speaker after speaker chimed in—and, as I said earlier, these were highly visible spokesmen for some of the largest and most prominent ministries in America—and, basically, they read Rove and his party the riot act.

One of the people who spoke up was Phil Burress, with Ohio Election Central. He told Rove that he and his associates had traveled the state of Ohio from one end to the other, and they had done the market studies that helped the Republicans win the election. He said they had seen the strong correlation between the beliefs of the people of Ohio and the marriage amendment on the ballot, and he told Rove that if that measure had not been included, the Republicans would have lost Ohio and the election.

But that did not mesh with the rhetoric Mr. Rove had invented. He listened for a while as one speaker after another spoke up, then he reacted indignantly. He thought he had been set up, and he seemed angry that we had spoken so honestly and openly. When the conversation was over, I think most of us doubted that he had even heard or understood what we were saying, and that has been the problem with the Republican leadership ever since the 2004 election.

Maybe they thought they had won the 2004 election on their good looks, but in 2006 they found out that was not enough. Those of us who were there that day had a better idea of what really happened at the polls. The arrogance and intransigence of Rove and the GOP leadership had fractured the conservative base and allowed the Democrats to take both houses of Congress. Later, when Karl Rove resigned his position on August 13, 2007, some in the media suggested it was the rats leaving a sinking ship. But I felt it had more to do with the Bush administration's loss of credibility with the people who had put them there.

Avoiding Social Laryngitis

In the days and weeks after that showdown in the White House, I continued thinking about all that had happened, and I felt I had a much better grasp on what had gone wrong in the Republican Party. The unity of the previous decade was broken, and the message that was going out seemed to be that the party's core conservative principles weren't all that important to those at the top.

For decades Democrats have accused Republicans of being tightfisted and cruel. The GOP, they said, is the party of rich white guys who can't spare a dime for the homeless, the poor, and the socially disadvantaged. They talk about morals on the campaign trail, but when it comes right down to it, they are as venal and self-serving as the next guy. It was politically motivated and an unfair characterization. But if that was the message the GOP strategists wanted to send, I had to say it was working.

The truth is, some elements of the Republican Party may need to apologize for not being as compassionate as they could have been, but as a rule, the men and women who make up the base of the party are much more generous than the liberals who claim to be so caring and compassionate. I have done extensive research on this subject and written about it in other books, and the facts are well documented.

One of the best new studies comes from Syracuse University professor Arthur Brooks. In his book, *Who Really Cares?* Brooks reports that conservatives who practice their religion, live in traditional nuclear families, and reject the notion that government should engage in income redistribution, turn out to be the most generous people in America. How much more generous? Brooks writes that homes headed by a conservative gave 30 percent more money to charity in 2000 than liberal families. On the other hand, secular liberals who believe in government handouts and taxpayer-funded entitlement programs turn out to be far less charitable. Liberals, he says, prefer to be generous with other people's money.[3]

Brooks also discovered that religious upbringing plays a key role in the degree of generosity people exhibit. And, as an added benefit, he found that those who give regularly to charities are, on average, happier and healthier than those who don't. In the foreword to the book, Brooks, who is a former Democrat and currently a registered Independent, makes this remarkable statement: "For too long, liberals have been claiming they are the most virtuous members of American society. Although they usually give less to charity, they have nevertheless lambasted conservatives for their callousness in the face of social injustice."[4]

The irony of those words cannot be missed. Even if conservatives are more generous, we ought to apologize for our narrow-mindedness on some occasions and for not rebuking the Republican Party for their sins. For a long time, those of us who have supported the Republican platform because of our moral convictions found ourselves in the position of defending the unrighteous and ungodly. We stand for something higher than what the merely political interests of the party were promoting, and for too long we seemed to be going along with it.

If we are going to be "the conscience for the nation," as I believe we ought to be, the evangelical community needs to stand for truth above all else. Otherwise we will be in danger of developing social laryngitis, and nobody's going to hear what we have to say about anything anymore. That is something else we want: we want the truth to make a difference.

RESURRECTED INFLUENCE

I have used the term "resurrected influence" from time to time in my sermons and writings to indicate my strong sense that the religious Right is not dead, as some have claimed. There are many current books and articles declaring that the influence of the religious Right has dissipated, and that with the passing of leaders like Jerry Falwell, D. James Kennedy, Bill Bright, and others, the conservative base is now defunct. With the defeat of the GOP in the 2006 midterm elections, they say, whatever steam was still left in the Christian Right has evaporated.

Fortunately, that is not the case. When I speak of resurrected influence, I am saying, "We did it once; we can do it again." When we get past the 2008 election, I hope we will be able to say, "We did it once, and we *did* it again." The evidence for this is strong, but the study from Market Strategies that I mentioned earlier provides some compelling new information about the changing electorate.[5]

What we find is that not only is the religious Right not dead, but the coalition of conservative voters who are motivated by faith and values continues to grow, so that today we are seeing large numbers of African American Christians who have traditionally supported the Democratic Party crossing over to the other side, voting for morally conservative Republican candidates. This is a phenomenon that is changing the canvas of politics in America, and I predict that it is going to be "the big story" for years to come.

At the end of the 2000 election controversy, when George Bush was confirmed as president despite the claims of Al Gore and the Democrats, all the usual suspects showed up to claim there had been voter fraud and intimidation at the polls. Then again in 2004, others showed up in Ohio, expecting to find all sorts of voting irregularities and eager to prove that blacks had been denied our right to vote.

Congressman John Conyers wrote a whole book about it, in fact, in which he claimed that the Klan was on the march again in America, and African Americans were being threatened and disenfranchised en masse.[6] There was no basis to the claim, and later investigations confirmed the results of both those elections. Despite all the controversy about hanging chads in 2000, it was proved repeatedly that Bush had won fair and square. The Democrats could not explain the anomaly, and they could not accept the fact that such a large number of blacks and Hispanics had crossed over and voted for the Republicans. That is why they went on the attack.

At one point, the rabble-rousers tried to make a case that Ken Blackwell, the conservative black secretary of state in Ohio who campaigned to become the first black governor of the state, had manipulated the vote count. What actually happened is that the Democratic Party was outstrategized by a unique collaboration of white evangelicals and the "new black church," who recognized that their issues were synonymous with those of their white Christian counterparts.

SQUANDERING THE ADVANTAGE

What happened next is a flash point for me. The liberal media were so enflamed by the changing face of the conservative movement that they immediately went on the attack against the special interest groups they felt had tampered with the electorate. Democrats had been counting on a big win, and it now appeared that a substantial number of minority voters had changed horses in midstream. Everyone from Bill Moyers on PBS to liberal columnists like Frank Rich in the pages of the *New York Times* jumped on the bandwagon, trying to stir up fear and resentment against the religious Right.

It was the old idea of "divide and conquer," and angry journalists were trying to say that the election was rigged and the vote had been manipulated. But the Republicans had not cheated—this was confirmed countless times by independent investigators—and they didn't have to tailor their message to each group. They had one message, limited government, and they were going to make things better for the individual through economic reforms. But the foundation of the Republican platform was their emphasis on moral values, pro-life issues, and a constitutional amendment defining marriage as the union of a man and a woman.

That was the reason for their victories in 2000, 2002, and 2004: the moral message. But when they abandoned their emphasis on those issues in the 2006 election, they were suddenly vulnerable once again. It took away the stickiness factor for the African American voters who had crossed over to support the moral agenda of the GOP. But even so, the margin of victory for the Democrats in 2006 was surprisingly small. Some congressional races were decided by the slimmest of margins—often no more than a few thousand votes. Most of the Democrats who were elected were moderates with socially conservative leanings.

Some of them, like Bob Casey in Pennsylvania and Heath Shuler in North Carolina, were forced to demonstrate how similar they were in their views to the Republicans on social issues in order to win. In other words, even with the defection of values voters who felt abandoned and the resistance of a large number of voters who were angered by the president's position on border security and illegal immigration (which was substantial), the Democrats' margin of victory was still barely enough to wrest control of Congress away from the GOP. These trends showed up in the polls from CNN, *Newsweek*, the *Wall Street Journal*, and others at the time.

When Karl Rove and the GOP strategists turned their backs on the base of black and white conservative voters, they either made a huge tactical blunder or they intentionally threw the election. I don't really believe it was really the latter, although I would not rule it out. But knowing how all these things happened does shed some light on the results of the 2006 election. It ought to remind everyone how important this alignment of black, white, and Hispanic conservatives can be.

Media pundits and the talking heads on cable TV had been saying for years that Karl Rove was the evil genius behind the Bush presidency. But what happened in 2006 tells us that Rove didn't get it. Until that time, black conservatives were moving into alignment with the conservative moral message from the White House. They got it, and the leaders of the new black church were saying that genuine faith ought to affect all our actions, and that voting is an important part of being a faithful and responsible Christian.

This is why the Republicans won big in the 2002 midterm elections and held on to both houses of Congress and the White House in the 2004 general election. Bush won in 2004 by the slimmest of margins in Florida and Ohio, and that victory had to be attributed to the number of black voters who cast their ballots for the candidates who most clearly reflected their views. But because there was mostly only lip service for them in Karl Rove's game plan in 2006, they felt jilted and went the other way. The defeat that followed was inevitable.

If the GOP leadership had stuck to their promises to religious conservatives and mounted a moral-values campaign, I have to believe they would have retained both the House and the Senate in 2006. That would have been a historic accomplishment since, as I said earlier, the party in power always loses seats in off-year elections. But the confusion was not limited to the politicians, because the media utterly missed this critical dynamic and went straight back to their old divide-and-conquer routine, claiming, "The religious Right is dead."

Some of the networks produced whole hour-long segments claiming that Christian conservatives have lost their punch and the right-wing agenda is clinically dead. But they could not be more wrong. The reactions of Christian conservatives determined the outcome of the elections. Their support had kept the Republicans in power, and their rejection of the GOP's compromises in 2006 sent them packing. When the base is energized behind candidates who understand and who are tuned in to the message, great things can happen. For now, the base is still disaffected, because we have lost faith in the Republican Party. But it does not have to stay that way forever.

THE MISSING PAGE

The Republican defeat in the 2006 election was an eye-opener. By the time President Bush delivered his State of the Union address the following year on January 23, 2007, his supporters were anxious to hear what he would say and how he would say it. We had a lot of questions about the integrity of the administration by this time, and we were eager to know if the White House had actually reneged on its long-standing relationship with the evangelical base. If not, this would be a good time to reaffirm the party's commitment to traditional values. If they wanted to take advantage of this historic confluence of black, white, and Hispanic conservatives, this would be the place to do it.

Everyone said the speech was well rehearsed, clear, and cogent. Some said it was the president's best effort since entering the White House in January 2001. In fact, a story in the *Washington Times* ran under the headline, "President's Union Speech Pleases Conservative Base." This article went on to say that most conservatives were happy with the message. The tone and demeanor of Bush's delivery showed strength and resolve.

And some who had doubted his commitment to the conservative agenda were confident the president wasn't going to abdicate his strong leadership role.[7]

I admit I was impressed too when the president took a moment to recognize a remarkable African athlete, Dikembe Mutombo, who is the star center for the Houston Rockets basketball team. Mr. Bush asked him to stand in the House gallery and said, "Dikembe became a star in the NBA, and a citizen of the United States. But he never forgot the land of his birth, or the duty to share his blessings with others. He built a brand new hospital in his old hometown. A friend has said of this good-hearted man, 'Mutombo believes that God has given him this opportunity to do great things.'" The president concluded by saying, "We're proud to call this son of the Congo a citizen of the United States of America."[8]

It was a moving tribute on a number of levels, and once again I was hopeful that President Bush would recognize the importance of the conservative base. After all, here was a black African superstar who was using his affluence, his influence, and his Christian faith to make a difference for hurting people in his native land. Unfortunately, while there were many things to applaud in the 2007 speech, most evangelicals had to wonder if anything had really changed. Many who had been among the president's most loyal supporters felt left out because he hardly mentioned any of the issues we cared about. Once again, it seemed the president was backing away from the issues he had championed two years earlier. What troubled us most was not what the president said but what he did not say.

When Tony Perkins was asked to comment on the address this time, he said, "I applaud the president's leadership. He refused to surrender his role of commander-in-chief to the new majority. However, I believe the president failed to challenge the new majority to advance core family and cultural issues, issues that many in the new majority campaigned on last year. These same issues will motivate pro-family Americans to rally around an administration that needs support."[9]

Over the years, evangelical organizations have been unwavering in their support for the president. And even though they had delivered huge numbers of votes for the GOP, suddenly many were feeling unheard and neglected. Some evangelical leaders said they felt as if they had painted themselves into a political corner, and a few even spoke of the possibility of the most feared option, a third-party challenge. It was an option no one really wanted, but I felt that some of the most vocal Christian leaders were using it as a threat to encourage the Republican leaders to think carefully about what they were doing.

A Troublesome Report

Both blacks and whites had received more lip service than results from politicians in recent months, and suggesting the possibility of a third-party united on their core issues had to be seen as a genuine and viable threat. Most evangelicals still believe the president has been honest about his deeply held Christian beliefs. However, some of the faithful are beginning to question the wisdom of the party leaders. Others have suggested the GOP merely used the faith issues to add another large constituency to the fold without any deeper commitment.

One of those was former White House staffer David Kuo, whose kiss-and-tell book, *Tempting Faith*, added fuel to the fire by calling the GOP's courtship of evangelical voters a political seduction.[10] In describing his final conversation with former White House Chief of Staff Andrew Card as he was leaving his position in the Office of Community and Faith-Based Initiatives, Kuo writes that the meeting was supposed to be a standard exit interview. It was to be short and sweet and complimentary in tone. But after all he had seen and done, Kuo says, he knew he had to say something about the actual environment he had worked in.

"I had been through too much not to say something," writes Kuo. "I told him everything I thought. The president had made great promises but they hadn't been delivered on. Worse than that, the White House hadn't tried. Worse than that, we had used people of faith to further our political agenda and hadn't given them anything in return." Furthermore, when referring to the faith-based program, he told Card that he had often heard White House staffers speaking of the office in the most vulgar terms.

Even before the book hit the bookstores, Kuo was bombarded with interview requests from the major news media. He was featured on a widely promoted segment of the CBS News feature *60 Minutes*, in which he laid out the dirty laundry. Subsequently he was on *Good Morning America*, *Larry King Live*, a PBS special, National Public Radio, MSNBC, FOX News, and dozens more. He was even interviewed by Tavis Smiley on BET and was repeatedly quoted in both print and broadcast media, mainly for the one line the liberal press most wanted to hear—that evangelicals ought to back off and "take a fast from politics." As Kuo explained later, he felt it was time for Christian conservatives to reexamine their political involvement.[11]

What the president's opponents saw in Kuo's report was an opportunity to divide the base of the GOP—and what could be better than an opportunity provided by one of their own to split up the alliance between black and white Christians? What the evangelical community saw was just as troublesome because it seemed to confirm their own fears that the leadership of the party was simply taking advantage of "values voters" in order to secure their own positions, without any deeper commitment to the actual moral issues that originally brought them together.

Rather than dividing the base, these new revelations actually caused the Christian electorate to go back to their leaders, demanding greater accountability and responsiveness. Those who did back off temporarily to reexamine their political involvement came back better armed and better prepared than ever. On the macro level, the nation desperately needs the moral voice of the faith community. For that reason, many evangelicals are unwilling to withdraw from the political arena, even when there is evidence of duplicity. Time will reveal what was really going on in the White House at that time, but I tend to believe that the president was simply trying to juggle too many agendas—and not doing it very well.

A Confluence of Values

Tony Perkins had said much the same thing when he warned the White House, "It's time to stop juggling!" In his open letter to the president, he challenged the Bush administration to "lead based on your core principles." The mandate from the grass roots has never been more urgent than it is now. The Bush presidency is coming to an end, and the current Republican presidential aspirants are struggling to make a showing against the Democratic candidates who have the media on their side. The only way voters will understand what is truly at stake is if the candidates speak clearly with the full weight of the White House behind them.

If the GOP listens to what the base is saying, the new convergence of black, white, and Hispanic voters can be the critical difference in the upcoming elections. A grassroots alliance of blacks, whites, and Hispanics around socially conservative issues can literally transform the face of politics in America. Even if minority voters continue to give most of their support to the Democratic Party, the demand for a conservative moral agenda in both parties will be undeniable. And that could force Democrats and Republicans to begin working together in ways we haven't seen in many years.

If my assessment is correct, the president missed a great opportunity to create bipartisan traction on our issues. The administration's softer position on same-sex marriage, the sanctity of life, and a host of other social concerns has hurt them, although it may not be entirely their fault. The people who helped organize the marriage amendment could have done a better job. They made a lot of promises but were not very effective in mobilizing the voters. As in any large-scale political movement, there were all kinds of people in all kinds of coalitions—some more effective than others. Even so, the black community turned out more people who supported the marriage amendment than any other group.

Some of the groups that yelled the loudest turned out to be three miles wide and a half inch deep in terms of their grassroots support. Other evangelical leaders were very disciplined about what they did and offered excellent input, but they did not have the support they needed among either the movement conservatives or the broader voting public. In most cases they could speak effectively for the religious Right but could not take it much further than that. So the administration is not entirely to blame. We all could have done a better job.

No one ever said that coalition building would be easy, but the attacks from black leaders on the old civil rights bandwagon were the harshest. One outspoken critic, who is the director of political fundraising for the NAACP in New Jersey, accused African Americans who voted for GOP candidates of "a kind of political schizophrenia." In a widely distributed interview, he claimed the Republican strategy to appeal to black voters is "not to convert legions of blacks to the GOP, which would seriously dilute the party's white appeal...." Instead, he said, "The Right's real goal is to create the impression of fundamental splits in black ranks, and thus subvert the credibility of mainstream leaders who hold to the historical black political consensus."[12]

Conscience, moral choices, and honest concern for the decline of the traditional family, to his way of thinking, were not good enough reasons to support a morally conservative ticket. Black preachers who support these issues, he said, are merely "hustlers who are willing to advance the GOP project." So this man, who happens to be responsible for raising millions of dollars for the Democrats in the Northeast, said it is all about the money. "Money does the trick." It's not really a battle for the hearts and minds of black voters, he said, but a battle for their pocketbooks. And worst of all, it is "an assault on the historical unity of African Americans."

Fortunately, that cynical and disrespectful view did not go unnoticed. During the first week of February 2005, President Bush spoke to an audience of black clergy, veterans, business leaders, and members of Congress about the importance of our shared values.

The meeting, held in the East Room of the White House, was interrupted seventeen times by applause. Among those in attendance were Senator Barack Obama and Rep. Melvin Watt, who is a North Carolina Democrat and chairman of the Congressional Black Caucus.[13]

In the run-up to the 2006 midterm election, the administration sent teams of election specialists to conduct technical assistance workshops for civic and community groups in cities where there appeared to be a growing consensus of African American Christians and white conservatives. Republican National Committee Chairman Ken Mehlman hosted a series of outreach events with black leaders, in which he acknowledged that the percentage of black conservatives was larger than ever. "We're committed to continuing to grow that percentage," he said, "and we recognize that it's going to require a long investment." He also said, "I strongly believe that if we lay out our policies and lay out our vision, that we have a tremendous opportunity."[14] I believe he's right about that if those policies turn out to be the ones that brought us together in the first place. If not, the Republican leaders may be in for a big surprise.

What this new consensus of values voters is saying to Washington today is that we are listening and we are watching what you do. We care about the policies. And as long as the focus is strong on restoring our moral foundations, we will support that vision. But we also have a vision of our own—a vision born out of adversity that was expressed most profoundly by Martin Luther King Jr. on the steps of the Lincoln Memorial. It is a dream that one day righteousness and justice will come together in this land and that all God's children will live together in peace. That is what we really want.

PART II

TRUTH IN ACTION

CHAPTER SIX

The Elephant in the Room

D URING THE SPRING OF 2007, THE CNN TELEVISION NETWORK
devoted nearly five days of prime-time programming to discussions of the role of religion in America. Catholics, Protestants,
evangelicals, and Jews each had some representation. By my count
there were at least five different specials, each repeated strategically over the Easter holiday weekend. As a rule, CNN has not
been a particularly friendly venue for people of faith, so I doubt
if anyone watching those specials was expecting any accolades for
evangelicals. And, of course, there weren't any.

But no matter why the producers ventured out into these
troubled waters, CNN's religious coverage marks a noteworthy
departure from the television giant's typical *modus operandi*.
Evangelicals generally expect poor treatment and unfair stereotyp-
ing from these folks. This group of programs, however, seemed a
bit more evenhanded and objective in their journalistic approach.
At times they even seemed faith affirming and inspirational, and I
would suspect their response to the Easter season on this occasion
may have yielded many new viewers for the news channel, which
is no doubt what they were after all along.

The programs I saw ranged from quasi-documentary pieces to
issue-oriented discussions of controversial topics. One special was
a two-part series hosted by the network's popular news luminary
Anderson Cooper. The program, called "What Is a Christian?"

explored the tension between science and faith.[1] Segments were diverse, fast paced, and informative. The tone of each vignette was, for the most part, objective and civil, despite the occasional outburst of impassioned debate. Cooper himself displayed curiosity and openness to each presenter. One question in particular seemed to be the real concern, "How is the faith community in the U.S. changing in both force and focus?"

Another special that week was the documentary "What Would Jesus Really Do?"[2] The program was engaging, and the host, Roland Martin, was charming. Although this one was more overtly critical of the evangelical Christian movement, the host nevertheless asked important questions about evangelical views on issues such as global warming, the Iraq war, and the divide between rich and poor.

In the interviews used throughout the broadcast, Martin spoke with Bishop T. D. Jakes, Pastor Paula White, Pastor Rick Warren, Rev. Jerry Falwell, and other evangelical leaders. Without specifically saying that there are major differences between the majority of black evangelical clergy and their white counterparts, Martin, who is African American, allowed these new voices to present their positions on a variety of topics. I was pleased that he resisted the temptation to trot out Jessie Jackson and Al Sharpton as his preferred "black experts."

All in all, CNN is to be commended for their willingness to air these programs. They did a good job of presenting some of the foundational truths of Christian theology without giving in to the urge to assault our beliefs as old-fashioned and repressive. The one thing Cooper and company failed to pick up on, however, was that the Christian Right is in the process of transition as a generation of pioneer evangelical leaders is about to pass from the scene.

It is unlikely that secular liberal networks like CNN are suddenly anxious to appeal to the evangelical community. Programming decisions at these venues are not based on moral concerns but on simple mathematics. The bright programmers at these networks are aware of the fact that the faith community, along with subgroups such as "crunchy cons," "neocons," and "so-cons," have helped to catapult FOX News into the cable TV stratosphere. In the end, it is a game of numbers, and they can count. CNN is looking for a bigger audience for purely pragmatic reasons and hoping for a silver bullet to fire at their rivals over at FOX.

REMAINING TRUE TO THE WORD

It is amazing that the liberal media, which have been fearful of the religious Right, are venturing out into uncharted waters. Who knows what they may come up with next? Now that they have taken a few steps toward the faithful, maybe they will want to try and frame the religious debates in this country. Or maybe they will even try to interpret our culture and traditions, or weigh in on the political objectives of evangelicals. It is possible that some of these folks have had their eyes opened. But more than likely they have just counted noses and realized where the action is.

The real story making headlines today is that the evangelical movement, so often attacked by the liberal press in the past, is growing larger and stronger by the day, to the point that it can no longer be ignored or attacked in the same old ways. The Christian faith really is the elephant in the room. And helping to make that point are a host of new studies that reveal just how vibrant the conservative Christian movement has become—among blacks, whites, Hispanics, Asian Americans, and others.

One such study is a groundbreaking new survey from the Pulpit and Pew Research Center at Duke University, which begins by saying that large-scale participation by African Americans in megachurch congregations of two thousand or more members has been largely ignored by the media. This study of trends among black churches and black pastoral leadership reveals a resiliency and strength that previous studies had missed. The research also found that African Americans make up fully 25 percent of the more than twelve hundred megachurch congregations.[3]

The report disputes earlier studies that have reported a decline in African American church attendance. According to the Pew and

Pulpit study, the last quarter of the twentieth century witnessed an explosion of new growth in predominantly black megachurches. Sociologist Scott Thumma of the Hartford Institute for Religion Research adds that at least 12 percent of churches without a black majority have "a significant black presence among their regular attenders."

Despite the claims of "institutional weakness" in the megachurch movement made by some of the leaders of more traditional black churches, this report paints a hopeful portrait of what's happening for African American churches and their pastors. Black evangelicals reveal a "loyalty and depth of commitment to this institutional area that is not found in other sectors of society," according to research director Lawrence Mamiya, "even among white churches."

For years the evangelical movement has been accused of being antiblack, antifemale, antipoor, and antigay, but that is an unfortunate mischaracterization. From the beginning, the evangelical movement has embraced men and women from all walks of life, from all cultures and classes. What some people perceive as exclusionary may actually be the tendency among all groups of people to gravitate toward the environments where they feel most comfortable. There are more mixed-race congregations today than ever before, but what matters most is not race but how a particular worship experience touches our hearts and enriches our walk with God.

Women have always had a vital role in our churches, and especially in the megachurches and other predominantly black congregations where women often share in pastoral or other leadership duties. It is true that Christian doctrine opposes the practice of homosexuality, and churches that remain faithful to the Scriptures refuse Holy Communion to individuals who refuse to abide by biblical teaching on this subject. But that is not bigotry. It is simply being faithful to the Word of God, which was given to us "for our good," as the Bible says.[4]

That answer may not satisfy people who deny the authority of

Scripture, or who believe they have a right to pursue a lifestyle that even science and medicine have shown to be deadly and unnatural. But that is what conversion is all about. The religious Right is changing today in terms of race, gender, and age, but the foundational beliefs of our faith will never change. We are eager to reach out to anyone willing to confess their past mistakes and make a new beginning in Christ, which is the true meaning of repentance, but we cannot simply wink at sin.

The homosexual community rejects that message and accuses Christians of being hateful. But anyone who thinks the doctrine of grace is narrow-minded or bigoted is missing the point of salvation and the whole process of redemption through Christ's atonement. Jesus did not come to start a fan club; He came to save sinners and to offer them eternal life. But we have to come to Him on His terms.

Although the numbers are difficult to quantify, there is an enormous groundswell of new growth taking place in the church today, precisely because people are looking for truth they can trust in this confusing and chaotic culture. Millions of younger, multicultural converts are joining churches all over America and around the world, and these young people are tuned in to issues their parents and grandparents never thought much about. These new converts are more culturally aware and more politically engaged than the "values voters" of the last few years, which is one of the main reasons for the title of this book: I have written it as a resource for a generation of culturally sensitive believers who are looking for truth in black and white.

YOUTH ON THE MARCH

Groups like Teen Mania, headquartered in Garden Valley, Texas, are raising up a new generation of faithful believers. Their purpose is to "provoke a young generation to passionately pursue Jesus Christ and to take His life-giving message to the ends of the earth."[5] The group's founder is Rev. Ron Luce, who holds both bachelor's and master's degrees in counseling and psychology. In addition, he is a graduate of the Harvard Business School's Owner/President Management Program. This unique blend of management and ministry credentials has allowed Luce to create a sophisticated and dynamic organization.

The headline-grabbing events hosted by Teen Mania each year are the Acquire the Fire and Battle Cry weekends that bring teens together from all over the country to praise the Lord, pray, and hear words of challenge. In 2005, Luce and company conducted over thirty Acquire the Fire/Battle Cry events, with an estimated 250,000 young people in attendance. One of the most sensational, which provoked hostile counterdemonstrations by homosexual activists, was held at Ghirardelli Square in San Francisco. That event was spotlighted on the CBS *60 Minutes* news magazine. Another twenty-six events are scheduled for the first six months of 2008.

See You at the Pole (SYATP) is another movement that is investing in this young generation of future values voters. At this annual event, high school and junior high kids ages twelve to eighteen come together to form new relationships that will help them grow in their faith. The movement began in 1990 when a handful of teenagers gathered for a discipleship weekend in Burleson, Texas. The teens were burdened for their classmates and decided to meet at the flagpole one morning to pray for their school, their friends, and their families.

It was a moving experience, and before long they were joined by others who wanted to participate in intercessory prayer. After a while, that group joined with others, and together they started spreading the word all over the state. They arranged to meet at their school flagpoles at the same time on the same day to pray. From that point, the idea took off, and the first multistate See You at the Pole event took place on September 12, 1990. At seven o'clock in the morning, before the first bell, more than forty-five thousand students gathered around their school flagpoles in four states to pray.

After that, news of the student-led prayer movement spread

to youth ministers at a national conference held in Colorado the following year. Even though there were no plans for a second SYATP event at that point, it was clear that the students intended to create one. For their second meeting, more than a million students gathered on September 11, 1991, at flagpoles from Massachusetts to California. They prayed for their friends, schools, families, and leaders—and this time, with the focus of the entire world suddenly on the recent war in Iraq and Kuwait and mounting tensions in the Middle East, they prayed especially for their country.

See You at the Pole has continued to grow each year. Today, more than three million students from every state in the country take part, joined by students in more than twenty other nations around the world, including Japan, Turkey, Australia, and even the Ivory Coast in Africa. Paul Fleischmann, the president of the National Network of Youth Ministries, says, "Every year, we have seen this day serve as a springboard for unity among teenagers on their campuses.... Young people have taken unprecedented leadership through this to have a positive impact at their schools."[6]

These are just two examples of movements that are making news today.

GROWING THE CHURCH

In times of stress and uncertainty, people will generally look for something solid to hold on to. It is as true today as it has ever been, and in the midst of all the chaos and confusion of this modern era, more and more people are returning to their roots and discovering the consolation that can only come through a robust Christian faith. It is no secret that the so-called "mainline churches" in this country have been on the decline for some time. Episcopalian, Presbyterian, Methodist, Church of Christ, and many others, claiming to be more "tolerant" and "affirming" of behaviors and beliefs forbidden by Christian doctrine since the time of Christ, are racing toward irrelevance, while doctrinally sound congregations are experiencing a tremendous surge of new growth.

Confirming this point is a new study from LifeWay Research, a division of LifeWay Christian Resources, which shows that the evangelical church in America is thriving and growing larger and stronger than ever through the planting of new churches and outreach activities of large evangelical congregations. According to Ed Stetzer, who is research director at LifeWay, church planting is considered "a preferred ministry option" for church leaders and laymen and a primary ministry focus for reaching the lost. These are among the conclusions of one of the largest and most comprehensive studies of church planting ever conducted.[7]

The "The State of Church Planting USA" report found that interest in church planting is growing rapidly in this country, and the pace has accelerated dramatically with as many as four thousand new congregations established in the United States each year. Stetzer's analysis also suggests that church planting is more varied than in the past, with "missional," "seeker-sensitive," "purpose-driven," and "ethnic" church-planting models leading the way. Furthermore, these new and uniquely twenty-first-century churches produce more conversions than conventional churches.

Twenty years ago, most church-planting activities were focused on geography and reaching new areas and "unserved" communities, whereas today churches are formed based on "affinity group" strategies. Dave Travis, managing director of the Dallas-based Leadership Network, which cooperated with Stetzer's group in the study, told the *Christian Post Reporter,* "I think a lot of it is demographically driven." He added that "most successful church planters today are specialists who emphasize a particular style of worship or a specific demographic."[8]

As one example, he said, they may exclusively plant house churches or ethnic churches, or they may focus more on purpose-driven, seeker, or missional church models. This trend toward specialization is likely to continue as more tools and resources that serve these specific types of planting strategies are developed.

Debunking the claims of traditionalists that most new churches fail within the first year, this study shows that survival and success of new church plants are actually greater than anyone realized. The latest research suggests that 68 percent of the approximately four thousand new church plants are still functioning four years later.

This rash of activity is not happening because there are not enough churches to choose from; it is happening because the churches many folks have to choose from are not dealing with the issues that concern men and women today. The more wishy-washy the mainline churches become, the more today's savvy young professionals are looking for that solid rock of truth. These new churches are focused on worship and clear and concise biblical teaching, and that is why they work. "Church planting has grown in its scope, diversity and impact," says Ed Stetzer. "North American churches, networks and denominations are making church planting a growing priority. Such emphases push the church closer toward a movement, where churches plant churches that plant churches across North America and the world."

CONCERNS ABOUT CULTURE

Another new study from the National Association of Evangelicals (NAE), headquartered in Washington DC, reports that the number-one concern of Christians in America is how to deal with the changes in American culture. The NAE's annual survey of its members suggests that national politics and the war in Iraq are less important than the worries about consumerism, materialism, family finances, and the breakdown of the traditional family. These were listed as the top issues by evangelical leaders representing approximately thirty million members.[9]

The most troubling issue for evangelicals, as it has been for more than thirty years, is the issue of abortion and defending the sanctity of human life at all stages, including stem cell research and related new technologies. However, immediately after that, evangelical leaders said that caring for the poor and disadvantaged, including HIV/AIDS victims and families living in poverty, were primary concerns. A significant number, including Hispanic members of the NAE, listed immigration and border security as issues needing more attention.

The third most frequent response from members of the NAE board was evangelism and reaching out to nonbelievers with the gospel. The emphasis, they said, needs to be on keeping the Christian message as honest and simple as possible. They also said that increasing the credibility and integrity of Christians was an important concern, along with increasing the level of passion in our churches and speaking up about the freedom of religion in other countries.

It should come as no surprise that some of the leaders cited in the survey expressed concern about misrepresentations of evangelical faith and the tendency of the media to mischaracterize evangelicals as being mainly interested in politics rather than spiritual issues. In fact, evangelicals only became motivated to become engaged in the political arena when they realized that the secular culture was doing its best to eradicate religion from the public square and to seal off every expression of our Christian beliefs behind the walls of the church.

The Christian witness has been damaged in recent years by scandals among some of its most visible public figures, the respondents said. Not least among these were revelations emblazoned on the front pages of virtually every major newspaper in the country involving NAE president Ted Haggard, who resigned his position in disgrace when evidence of his solicitation of a male prostitute was made public. Subsequently, Haggard placed himself on administrative leave as senior minister of New Life Church in Colorado Springs, pending a church investigation, and was subsequently dismissed by the board of overseers when the allegations were found to be true.

The problems don't end with Ted Haggard, of course. In just the past several months we have learned of scandals involving members of the Senate and the House of Representatives, many of whom had campaigned as moral conservatives. The respondents to the NAE survey made frequent reference to the need for evangelicals to do a better job of living in accordance with the values and beliefs they represent, not only in their private lives but in their public lives as well. Coinciding right along with this was the fourth most frequent concern of that organization's members: restoring the definition and value of the term "evangelical."

CONCERN FOR THE ENVIRONMENT

In recent years, evangelicals have had strongly mixed reactions to the media's portrayal of global warming as a catastrophe in the making. The majority of Christian conservatives believe in the biblical view of stewardship, which is that we are to use the earth and its natural resources with care. We are taught to take care of our physical environment the same way we would take care of our homes and our neighborhoods, but the earth is not an object of worship, and there are some in the "environmental movement" who have taken it to that point.

Scripture teaches that God made man and woman in His own image and likeness and commanded us to "have dominion over the fish of the sea, over the birds of the air, and over the cattle, over all the earth and over every creeping thing that creeps on the earth" (Gen. 1:26). The teaching commonly referred to as "dominion theology" derives from that precept. This is also a principle of faith that has been mischaracterized by the mainstream media.

Evangelicals, as the NAE study suggests, may disagree about the cause and severity of global climate change, but there is general agreement that, as Christians, we are to care for the earth. Traditional teaching holds that we are to use the natural resources, including the animal kingdom, for our benefit, but we are not to destroy or misuse the environment in a careless fashion. No one disputes that there has been a minor increase in earth temperatures over the past century—perhaps as much as one-half degree Fahrenheit—but the primary dispute is whether or not the rise is man-made, from carbon emissions, or whether it is a natural cycle.[10]

According to a separate study by the Barna Group, only 33 percent of evangelical Christians see global warming as a major problem.[11] But the news in 2006 that eighty-six evangelical leaders had signed a document affirming the dangers of global warming and calling for a major initiative to reduce carbon emissions came as a shock to many believers. Among the signers were the presidents of thirty-nine evangelical colleges, the leaders of several Christian relief organizations such as the Salvation Army, and pastors of megachurches, including Rick Warren, pastor of the Saddleback megachurch in San Diego.[12]

The list also includes several well-known black leaders, such as Bishop Charles E. Blake Sr. of the West Angeles Church of God in Christ in Los Angeles, Rev. Floyd Flake of the Greater Allen A.M.E. Cathedral in New York City, and Bishop Wellington Boone of the Father's House and Wellington Boone Ministries in Norcross, Georgia. And Rev. Jesse Miranda, president of AMEN in Costa Mesa, California, signed the document as well.

Black leaders have tended to follow the Democratic Party position on this issue, while white evangelicals tend to be more skeptical. My own position is that we need to be careful about how we get involved in this dispute. The media and a lot of Hollywood superstars have been caught up in the movement with unrestrained passion, which, by itself, ought to make us a little suspicious. It is important to follow the science, but, honestly, the jury is still out on that. Claims made by spokesmen like former Vice President Al Gore, that 90 percent of all scientists believe global warming is a major crisis, are simply false. A powerful new report prepared by the British Broadcasting Company (BBC) in 2007 analyzes the discrepancies in the claims of the global-warming propagandists and concludes that global warming is a natural cyclical phenomenon that alternates with even longer periods of global cooling—and many scientists hold that view.

Most evangelicals tend to agree that caution is needed, especially when it comes to the enormous tax-and-spend measures attached to all the proposals currently being considered by the "experts." The evangelical statement on the environment mentioned above calls for new federal legislation, as well as demanding reductions in carbon emissions through what it calls "cost-effective, market-based mechanisms." But such mechanisms will necessarily include financial penalties and extensive federal regulations that could be disastrous for business and industry.

Other topics that ranked lower on the list of concerns in the NAE survey included health care, teaching of Christian doctrine, the promotion of homosexuality by the mainstream media, the rise of radical Islam, and the need for a renewed emphasis on racial reconciliation. According to Rev. Leith Anderson, who presented the survey results at a Washington press conference, "answers were so diverse that they were difficult to categorize." But he added, "Maybe that's the whole point—that evangelical leaders have a long list of concerns."[13]

African American Values

To take this assessment of the views and values of the evangelical community one step further, I want to look now at another important survey from the Pew Research Center that sheds new light on the attitudes of African Americans and reveals the concerns of blacks and whites regarding the culture, communities, and other cultural relationships with the African American community. Some of the findings are eye-opening.[14]

To begin with, researchers defined the term *values* at the beginning of the survey as "things that people view as important or their general way of thinking." By a ratio of two to one, survey respondents said that the values of poor and middle-class blacks have grown apart over the last ten years. However, surprisingly, most blacks said that the values of blacks and whites have grown more alike during the same span. Roughly one-fourth of blacks surveyed (23 percent) said that middle-class and poor blacks have a lot of values in common.

Interestingly enough, whites who were interviewed for this study agreed that the values of blacks and whites have become more alike over the past decade, and they also perceived that the values of middle-class and poor blacks have become less similar. Educated blacks were more likely than those with less education to say that the values gap has widened in the black community over the past decade. Less-educated blacks felt just the opposite.

Other questions dealt with attitudes concerning the standard of living in black communities. By looking at figures from the current population survey of the federal census, researchers found that the gap between black median household income and white median household income has narrowed slightly over the last three decades. In 2006, the report says, median household income of African Americans was 61 percent of white median household income, compared to 1976 when the median household income for blacks was 58 percent of white median household income. Median household income of African Americans rose to 65 percent of white median household income at the end of the 1990s, before dropping back a bit after the turn of the new century.

Regarding the issues of racial prejudice and discrimination, the study found that most blacks believe that racial discrimination is still a fact of life, with 67 percent saying that blacks "often or almost always" face discrimination when applying for a job. Another 65 percent said the same about renting an apartment or buying a house, and 50 percent felt discrimination when dining at restaurants or shopping. By contrast, whites were twice as likely to say that blacks rarely face bias in those situations. However, while most blacks say they see discrimination as widespread, fewer believe it is the main reason that many blacks cannot get ahead.

Fully 53 percent of African Americans said that people in their community who don't get ahead are responsible for their own situation, and just 30 percent said that discrimination is mainly to blame for their troubles. As recently as the mid-1990s, researchers found precisely the opposite point of view, with a majority of blacks saying that discrimination is the main reason for a lack of black progress. Majorities of both whites and Hispanics agreed that blacks who don't get ahead are mainly responsible for their own situation. Both African Americans and Hispanics strongly support "affirmative action" to help blacks get education and jobs. However, both groups expressed less support for "racial preferences," and only 39 percent of whites supported the idea of giving "special preferences to qualified blacks in hiring and education."

THE STATE OF BLACK CULTURE

On the culture front, researchers found that while a plurality of blacks say the portrayal of blacks in movies and on television has improved in the past decade, they tend to believe that these portrayals are generally more hurtful than helpful to society's image of blacks. The area where the majority of those surveyed expressed the most concern was in the area of popular culture, and a substantial majority said the influence of rap music and hip-hop has a much worse impact on society than the images we see of blacks in movies and television.

Both blacks and whites agreed that rap and hip-hop are a bad influence on African American young people, primarily because of the vulgar language, the negative portrayal of women, and the glorification of violence. Researchers noted, however, that there were significant gender differences in the responses to these questions, and they reflected different attitudes between blacks and whites. Surprisingly, white men were more likely than women to say that hip-hop and rap music are a bad influence. Among blacks, however, women were more likely than men to see it that way.

In assessing the principal findings of their study, the Pew researchers highlighted the fact that just 40 percent of those surveyed felt that things are better for blacks now than they were five years ago. On the other hand, 44 percent said they think life for blacks will be better in the future. This was another area where whites had a different view. While the majority of whites were less optimistic about progress in the black community, they were more

than twice as likely as blacks (56 percent) to believe that the situation for blacks in this country will be better in the future.[15]

Other gaps in perception between blacks and whites became
apparent in this study. Blacks, for example, have far less confidence
than whites in the basic fairness of the criminal justice system.
Blacks and whites expressed very little overt animosity toward
individuals of the other race. Approximately 80 percent of each
group expressed a favorable view of the other group, and more
than 80 percent in each group said they know a person of a different race whom they consider a friend.

Whom do these people admire? More than 87 percent named
Oprah Winfrey as an African American public figure they admire,
85 percent named Bill Cosby, and 76 percent indicated that 2008
presidential candidate Barack Obama is a good influence on the
black community. By contrast, the report indicates that just 17
percent of blacks felt that rap artist 50 Cent is a good influence.
Finally, it is worth pointing out that a surprisingly large number of
African Americans say they have lost confidence in the effectiveness
of some of the most visible leaders in the black community, including national political figures, the clergy, and the NAACP. A majority
of blacks still see these groups as either very or somewhat effective,
but the number saying "very" effective has declined since 1986.

WHOM DO YOU TRUST?

On November 7, 2007, I was one of several guests on the *Lehrer
News Hour* on PBS who had been asked to comment on the 2008
presidential sweepstakes and the recent endorsements by Pat
Robertson, Senator Sam Brownback, and others. My segment began
with a video clip of Robertson's endorsement of former Mayor
Rudy Giuliani. Then *News Hour* host Gwen Ifill began by talking
about the changing landscape of the campaign. I was impressed by
her understanding of evangelical perspectives and later discovered
that she is a pastor's daughter. So her knowledge of the evangelical
community comes from personal experience.

During the interview, I suggested that the views of Christian conservatives were not changing just because some of the well-known evangelical leaders had come out in support of one candidate or the other. In the two cases we discussed, I pointed out that, frankly, neither one represents the views of the vast majority of Christian conservatives. After leaving the studio that day, it crossed my mind that the evangelical movement has at least two advantages today that we have never had before. First, our candidates for the 2008 election are outspoken pro-family and pro-life conservatives. Second, the Democratic candidates, all of whom are pro-choice and pro–gay rights, will have to try to appeal to the values of the faith community in this election if they expect to have any chance of actually being elected.

I remember how surprised I was in 2004 to see blacks, whites, and Hispanics sitting together around a conference table, developing strategies to protect the institution of marriage. Through that effort, several new friendships were formed, and most of the coalitions that were launched at that time are still in place today. What concerned me at that time was the feeling that the members of the movement were united by their fears rather than by their dreams.

I believe it is possible to win an election by appealing to the fears of the voters. We certainly have enough to be afraid of in this era of terrorist bombers and drive-by shootings. But what we need most of all is a dynamic vision, or in Dr. King's words, a dream of righteousness and justice large enough to bring people together for a greater purpose. Appealing to fear seems to me to be the path of least resistance. Christians have been exhorted to vote their values, but we are still waiting for the leaders who can offer us a convincing dream big enough to capture the hearts of Bible-believing Americans.

As a local church pastor, I am responsible for raising substantial sums of money for building programs and special events of various kinds. As a result, I have learned a couple of things that have helped shape my view of politics. First of all, in order to raise funds and elicit the assistance of volunteers, it is essential to present a clear and well-articulated vision of what you have to offer. It must be a vision that will touch the hearts of those you intend to serve. Second, if the only motivation you give the potential donor is a message of fear, that well will go dry before you know it. Fear is a short-term motivator.

The conservative Christian movement was not the brainchild of some church or denomination or college of bishops. It was a catalytic movement led in the early stages by the impassioned voices of Christian leaders like Jerry Falwell, Pat Robertson, James Dobson, D. James Kennedy, and others. It was not because, as a *Washington Post* reporter once claimed, evangelicals are "poor, uneducated, and easy to command." People followed their lead because their words struck a resonant chord in their own spirits.

Many of today's reporters and political pundits speak as if the evangelical movement were some huge, monolithic institution, like an alien army on the march. That is not the case at all. It is nothing more or less than a movement of men and women who share, first, a concern for the decline of values in American culture and, second, a belief that spiritual and cultural renewal is still possible, if we can come together and work for change. What the leaders of the evangelical movement had to offer was a prophetic vision of reform and renewal.

So where does that leave Christian conservatives today? I would have to say that it leaves us right in the middle of the action. This is why CNN, CBS, PBS, and all the major secular media are talking about religion and moral values today. There is hardly a day that the headlines and news reports on television don't have something to say about faith or some aspect of religion. The media have realized that, like it or not, the evangelical Christian community is the elephant in the room, with enough power and size to help shape the future of this nation for the next hundred years.

As we approach the 2008 elections, the majority of values voters are still waiting for the candidate who will come forward and deliver a clear and prophetic vision of what can be done and what lies ahead. Recently the *Los Angeles Times* quoted *WORLD* magazine editor Marvin Olasky as saying that, "Anyone who talks about delivering the evangelical vote might as well apply for a job as a herder of cats."[16]

I believe that is a good insight, and it is true. But the reason it is true is not because our goals are limited to political power or merely deciding which party will deliver the most goodies, and it is not just because we are so cantankerous. Evangelical Christians are independent thinkers who are guided by their conscience and the moral concerns that come through faith in a loving Father. Our votes and our values are directed not by a political party but by an even greater vision of unity, born out of an abiding faith in the One who said, "You shall know the truth, and the truth shall make you free" (John 8:32).

■ ■ ■ ■

CHAPTER SEVEN

Freedom of Conscience

O N SEPTEMBER 25, 2006, I WAS ON THE SET OF THE *Washington Journal* news program, which is a daily feature of the C-SPAN television network. The program, as many cable viewers will know, includes phone calls and e-mails to the guests from Democratic, Independent, and Republican viewers around the country. In some cases, feedback is objective and encouraging, but sometimes the questions can be angry and offensive. In the course of an hour broadcast, many points of view are expressed, but it can be a challenge for those in the hot seat to respond respectfully to all the questioners, who generally have a point of their own to make.

The topic on this day was one of the hottest: religion in politics. My fellow guest, Rev. Romal Tune, is an ordained minister and Democratic Party activist who runs a politically liberal nonprofit organization called Clergy Strategic Alliances. It was a lively debate, but I came away from the studio that day deeply troubled by several things that happened.

In his opening salvo, my opponent tried to say that same-sex marriage and abortion are wedge issues for voters. He said that conservatives use both these issues as a way of polarizing the electorate, and he indicated that fair-minded folks, like himself, of course, tried to avoid these kinds of controversial topics in order to "keep the political peace." There were so many holes in his argument that I was hard-pressed to respond to him in a civil manner. But it was apparent that this clergyman was speaking from the pro–gay marriage, proabortion script of his party.

The goal of gay-rights activists is to gain not just equal protection under the law, which is everyone's right guaranteed by the Fourteenth Amendment to the Constitution, but also special rights for homosexuals. It is not really about tolerance, as they often claim, but about acceptance and legitimization of an immoral lifestyle—enforced ultimately by an act of Congress. One of the major beachheads of the gay agenda, as their own literature states, is to gain "legal recognition for a wide range of relationships, households, and families, and for the children in all of those households and families, including same-sex marriage, domestic partner benefits, second-parent adoptions, and others."[1] These objectives are spelled out in detail, and this language can be found on homosexual Web sites such as BeyondMarriage.org.

The *Washington Blade*, a newspaper for homosexuals in the District of Columbia, often reports candidly on the activities and objectives of the gay community, and in one such report published around the time of my C-SPAN appearance, the newspaper described plans to bring gay leaders to Washington from all over the country to strategize new ways to enlist nongay people in their cause. The article indicated that sixteen national organizations were expected to participate, along with several groups that promote the homosexual agenda under the banner of "civil rights."[2]

The well-known homosexual activist attorney Evan Wolfson defined the purpose of the meeting by saying, "It's really less about a meeting and more about what we are doing to enlist nongay people and to move public opinion." The objective, he said, was to get a million people to sign a petition that states, "I support the right of every American to marry, including gay, lesbian, bisexual, and transgender couples. I believe that marriage and other civil rights protections are essential to making all families safer and more secure."[3]

THE CIVIL RIGHTS CANARD

As an African American, I am offended by that kind of language. Homosexuality has never been a civil right, and the heroes of the civil rights movement of the last century would be outraged that anyone would make such a claim. What gay activists are trying to do is to obscure what is actually involved—which is a lifestyle that is not only deadly but has also been forbidden by every civilized society in history—by hiding behind the legitimate banner of the civil rights movement.

The laws enacted by Congress during a century of struggle for equal rights for African Americans—from the 1860s through the 1960s—were intended to eliminate discrimination on the basis of race, not on the basis of an individual's sexual preferences. Race is a natural and inborn characteristic; it is not something we choose. Race is benign and tells us nothing about the character of the person. Homosexuality, on the other hand, is a choice. Despite the unfounded arguments of the gay community that homosexuality is determined at birth, there is no science to support that argument. Every claim by sympathetic researchers, publicized in the liberal media, that science has found a "gay gene" has been discredited and disproved.[4]

Furthermore, every adult in this country already has the constitutional right to marry. But there are, for good and proven reasons, certain restrictions. For example, you may not marry a child, a close relative, or a person who is already married to someone else. And you may not marry someone of the same sex. This is not prejudice but a sound legal precaution to protect society, and also to protect the individuals involved and their potential offspring from the disabilities and suffering that would naturally ensue from such relationships.

Gay activists claim that anyone who tries to limit their right to marry is trying to impose their religion on other people. But this is another deliberate misstatement. Defining marriage as the union of a man and a woman is not something invented by the Christian Right. There has never been any civilization in all of human history, until very recently, that would have considered homosexual relationships remotely equivalent to marriage. Marriage is not just a civil or religious agreement entered into by a husband and wife; it is the oldest covenant known to man, instituted by God for our own good.

No society in history—not even the most primitive and pagan cultures—has considered sexual relations between two men or two women comparable to the institution of marriage. Most have considered it a dangerous and immoral violation of nature. In 2005, this view was affirmed by the legislature of the state of New Hampshire, which issued a declaration saying that marriage "across essentially all societies and history has been defined as the union of a man and a woman." Their report said further that "marriage models both natural human sexuality and reproduction that commits to the health, safety, and welfare of both the individual and the community."[5]

After some sixteen months of hearings and testimony from a wide range of citizens, experts, and advocates of all persuasions, New Hampshire lawmakers concluded that maintaining the historic definition of marriage was in the best interest of the people of that state. But they also noted that, unlike sexual preference, a person's race is an immutable and innate characteristic. Racial equality was made a civil right under the Thirteenth, Fourteenth, and Fifteenth Amendments to the Constitution, but same-sex "marriage" has never been accorded such a right, they wisely concluded.

The Homosexual Lobby

In the fall of 2004, I met with a group of one hundred sixty African American bishops, pastors, ministers, evangelists, and other religious leaders in Washington who came together to call on Congress to take a principled stand in defense of traditional marriage. We wanted members of Congress to make it clear that attempts by homosexual activists to revise the nation's laws and devalue this time-honored institution were not an issue of civil rights but, in fact, a slap in the face to black families.

When we spoke to members of the Congressional Black Caucus (CBC), I honestly believed that this group of African American legislators would be responsive to our point of view. We were asking them to support a federal marriage amendment to insure that marriage would be protected. We pointed out that more than 74 percent of the African Americans who had been polled on the issue of same-sex marriage said they wanted to protect the institution of marriage as the union of one man and one woman.

In a written statement that we presented to the members of the CBC, we said, "It's no secret that black families have been under assault in recent years. Divorce, teenage pregnancy, fatherless homes, and a disproportionate number of HIV-AIDS cases are all unattractive aspects of the black family landscape. In addition, new research shows that there are already clear signs of long-term marital breakdown of the black family.... Two out of every three newborn blacks enter the world with an unwed mother and no consistent father figure." And we told them that the vast majority of black pastors and church leaders were in agreement with us that "further destabilization of traditional marriage must be prevented at all costs."

Unfortunately, the liberal bias of those public officials was too much to overcome. Instead of acknowledging the truth of our arguments, they accused us of bigotry and insensitivity to the gay community. They even let the civil rights issue pass without challenge. Representative John Lewis, an outspoken Georgia Democrat and a former associate of Martin Luther King Jr. during the civil rights era, stood up and said, "I just want to set the record straight here. Some of these so-called black ministers and so-called civil rights leaders never supported civil rights. They never marched one day. They never put their bodies on the line for the cause of civil rights." And he added imperiously that, "Coretta Scott King, the widow of Martin Luther King Jr., is opposed to this amendment."

I think that was an eye-opener for many of those present. We hadn't realized just how much our own black leaders had bought into the agenda of the gay community and their supporters in the Democratic Party. Eventually, six members of the Black Caucus did vote to support a marriage amendment, but it wasn't because they agreed with the logic of our appeal. It was because the voters in their home districts made it clear they expected them to step up and support the amendment to protect marriage.

I learned later that the office of Representative Harold Ford, a black congressman from Tennessee, received more than four thousand phone calls from constituents, and Representative William Jefferson's office in New Orleans received between four and five thousand phone calls. That is what made the difference. But I was saddened to think that the influence of homosexual activists apparently meant more to those Democratic leaders than the wishes of our people.

To add insult to injury, we found that there is a five-point plan in place to block any future legislation prohibiting homosexual marriage. They told us in morally condescending tones that the war in the Middle East, rising gas prices, and border security were the issues they ought to be focusing on, not whether or not gays should be allowed to marry. I am sure they used that sort of language to try to make us feel petty and bigoted.

But Damien Lavera, a spokesperson for the Democratic National Committee who deals specifically with gay and lesbian issues, spelled out the agenda of the homosexual lobby in an article in the *Washington Blade*. He said the DNC's "five-point plan" for fighting state ballot initiatives aimed at banning same-sex marriage is already working. The first step, he said, is to label all such ballot measures as "divisive ploys" used by Republicans to distract voters from more important issues, such as "the Bush's administration's failed policies."

Another, he said, consists of the "party-building" operations in states where homosexual marriage is an issue. These efforts would include training Democratic Party operatives in all fifty states in how to campaign against so-called "anti-gay ballot measures." Other elements of the plan, Lavera said, included working with the homosexual activist group, National Stonewall Democrats, to "develop strategy and talking points" regarding homosexual ballot measures;

working with campaign organizations to fight pro–traditional marriage ballot measures in each state; providing campaign advice, expertise, and logistical and financial support; and to "empower and organize GLBT communities around the country" through the help of the Democratic Party's "gay outreach" organizer.[6]

FULLY COMPROMISED

Despite the rhetoric of Democratic legislators who claim to be objective on these issues, it is apparent that they are fully compromised and working feverishly behind the scenes on their party's antimarriage agenda. Their language is always well rehearsed. It is amazing how the exact same words and phrases pop up in every conversation and press clip. Unfortunately, most of them lie to the public about their real motives. The reason they don't want to discuss the need for a constitutional amendment to protect marriage is because they would have to cross the party line to do so.

The Democratic National Committee decided to make the protection of marriage a Republican issue. Even though they have tried repeatedly to use the issue to discredit Republicans by illustrating how cruel and closed-minded we are, they inadvertently let the Republican Party take ownership of this issue as the protectors of traditional family values. That has been a tremendous blessing for conservatives. Values voters who came to the polls to support marriage in 2004 voted for Republican candidates, which became painfully obvious to the Democrats in the results from Ohio and Florida.

The Democratic Party could have chosen to support the two-parent family and stand up for traditional marriage. If they had taken a strong position in defense of traditional marriage, it could have splintered the Republican base. In fact, I have been told that President Clinton, who is a masterful strategist (whatever else you may think of him), offered Senator Kerry a winning strategy during his 2004 campaign. It was simply to declare that he wanted to protect traditional marriage, while offering homosexuals certain basic "civil rights" concessions.

If the rumor is true, that advice could have diffused the moral rebellion against the Democratic Party and handed Kerry a monumental victory. But Kerry decided instead to pander to the far-Left base of the party, while attempting to deceive mainstream voters about his true feelings on the issue. Democrats have continued with this approach ever since, even though they are losing support and alienating a huge number of morally conservative African American voters in the process.

In order to pretend that they still care about our values, they trot out candidates such as Senator Barack Obama, Representative Harold Ford, and other African Americans who talk about their spirituality and their support for the moral agenda. But no one is fooled by the rhetoric: the Democratic Party has abandoned the values voters. I predict that when the moderate democratic base truly understands the magnitude of their compromise, there will be a tremendous backlash at the polls.

The overwhelming majority of Americans believe strongly that marriage is the union of one man and one woman. The only reason the issue is even being discussed today is because a relatively small group of homosexual activists has gone to court, trying to find a few sympathetic judges who will listen to their arguments and, by fiat, subvert the laws of the nation. There is no way the American people would ever condone such fundamental changes in our laws if the issue ever came to a vote. But, with the aid and comfort of liberal judges in Vermont, Massachusetts, California, and other places, along with the subterfuge and collaboration of the leadership of the Democratic Party, the long march of gay activists through the institutions of American culture is under way. But the battle is far from over.

LEGISLATING INEQUALITY

As a sophomore in high school, I was fortunate enough to make the first string of my high school football team. But at some point in my first season, I took a painful helmet blow to the thigh that caused me to hobble for months. I began to think the injury would never go away. I would be fine one week, but then the pain would return, and I would be right back where I started. The injury obviously affected my performance on the field. I eventually made it through the season and went on to have several more. But I'm often reminded of that experience when I think about all the attempts that have been made by liberals to redefine the civil rights movement.

The radical demonstrations of the sixties are a thing of the past, and that is a good thing. But I have not given up on the civil rights movement, and I don't think we have accomplished all our goals yet. As I said early in these pages, we have seen progress in race relations, but we haven't seen the fulfillment of Dr. King's vision for America. It is true; we are not on the plantation anymore, and we have achieved a great deal since the sixties. There have been many improvements in racial relations over the years. But King's dream of a unified nation living together peacefully, with liberty and justice for all, has not been fulfilled.

The black community needs reviving, and the civil rights movement can help. But if the civil rights movement is co-opted by liberals and political activists who want to tear down the moral framework of the nation, then we are in for a long and bitter struggle. Like Bill Cosby, I believe that family formation is the most important issue facing the black community today. That word is getting out. But just as we are about to get the message across, homosexual activists are attempting to hijack the civil rights movement and turn it into something it is not.

What it really comes down to is an attempt by homosexuals to disguise their personal lifestyle choices as a civil rights issue. The degree to which the homosexual lobby depends on subterfuge and misrepresentation was spelled out in the now-infamous words of two of the early leaders of the movement. In an article called "Overhauling Straight America," published in a homosexual magazine, they said:

> You can forget about trying to persuade the masses that homo-
> sexuality is a good thing. But if only you can get them to think
> that it is just another thing with a shrug of their shoulders,
> then your battle for legal and social rights is virtually won.
> And to get to shoulder-shrug stage, gays as a class must cease
> to appear mysterious, alien, loathsome and contrary. A large-
> scale media campaign will be required in order to change the
> image of gays in America.[7]

Their goal then and now is to enforce acceptance and legitimization of their lifestyle, and to vilify and stigmatize anyone who
dares to stand in their way. In the same article, the writers go on to
describe several tactics that homosexuals can use to change public
opinion. The suggestions included:

1. Talking about gays and gayness as loudly and as
   often as possible
2. Portraying gays as victims, not as aggressive
   challengers
3. Giving protectors a just cause
4. Making gays look good
5. Making the "victimizers" look bad.

To make those who object to the homosexual lifestyle look
bad, they said, homosexuals were to use words, images, and slurs
comparing their opponents to Nazis, Klan members, and "igno-
rant homophobes." The object wasn't to convince or persuade but
to destroy their opponents by linking them to racists and "right-
wing crazies." If that sounds like all-out war, it is because that is
exactly what it is.

BAD LAWS AND BAD POLICY

The radical gay rights movement wants to silence the voice of the
church, which has been so strong on this issue. I observed this

two-pronged attack recently at a press conference I hosted in Washington on behalf of the High Impact Leadership Coalition. For several months, homosexual activists and their collaborators in the House of Representatives had been working to pass H.R. 3685, euphemistically called "The Employment Non-Discrimination Act," or ENDA.

As we began the meeting, I explained that the individuals taking part in that event represented a multicultural, multiracial group of Christians who believe that the so-called "hate crimes" legislation passed recently by the Senate, S. 1105, threatened to take this nation in a very dangerous direction. I said that we were grateful that President Bush had pledged to veto the legislation if it passed both houses of Congress. But we felt it was vitally important to stop the measure before it went any further.

Among those I had invited to participate in the press conference were representatives from the Family Research Council, Exodus International (a ministry to former homosexuals), the Let Freedom Ring Foundation (a religious liberties defense group), and Vision America. All of these nonprofit groups operate with a biblical mandate to protect and preserve the family, and to stand up against those groups and individuals who are trying to break the resolve of the American people on this issue.

Throughout the press conference there were individuals in the room who tried to discredit what we were saying by accusing us of using the same kinds of discrimination that has been used against blacks. Whenever anyone uses the term *discrimination*, it brings a bad taste to our mouths, and the homosexual activists know that. They have decided that this is the best way to reframe the debate, and aggressive activist groups cry discrimination as a way of attacking the church. By hijacking the language of civil rights, they are infringing on the liberties of everyone else.

Several African American speakers at the press conference took issue with the suggestion that blacks are in favor of pro-homosexual legislation, such as ENDA. It is true that some blacks who are wedded to the Democratic Party have spoken in favor of these laws, but the black community is no longer a one-party monolith. One size does not fit all. Even if some well-known civil rights leaders have sold out and supported the gay agenda, on that day we declared that we were strongly against it, and we were not about to let gay activists hide their intentions behind the issue of civil rights.

We spelled out our reasons for rejecting the ENDA bill and pointed out that such measures are meant to overturn the historical basis of protected-class status by adding the words "actual or perceived sexual orientation." While every other federally protected class embodies three standards—an obvious, immutable characteristic, a history of discrimination evidenced by economic disenfranchisement, and political powerlessness—"sexual orientation" meets none of these criteria. Furthermore, it's an insult to African Americans to grant special protections for "sexual orientation."

Secondly, the proposed legislation would expand civil rights protections on the basis of "perception." An employee or potential employee could then sue an employer for his or her perception of their sexual orientation. Unlike the recognized protected classes—race, age, and gender—sexual orientation is not scientifically verifiable. And, once again, it is an offense to African Americans to equate sexual orientation with skin color.

We also pointed out that nondiscrimination laws based on sexual orientation infringe on religious liberties. As Christian leaders, we cannot be expected to give up the rights of free speech and freedom of religion guaranteed by the Constitution. We should not be forced to ignore our deeply held convictions, and our parishioners should not be forced to disguise their beliefs when they leave the church. Such laws require people of faith to lay down their religious freedom at the door, and that is unacceptable.

Many African American churches have outreach ministries to serve the local community that are separate from the church. My local church, for example, runs a day-care center, which looks after more than two hundred children each day, with the potential to serve another hundred through extended after-school care.

According to the language in nondiscrimination laws such as the ENDA bill, child-care ministries, after-school programs, and all our food and clothing bank operations would suddenly be vulnerable to whatever unreasonable and unconstitutional demands the law might stipulate.

Any way you look at it, these laws are a direct attack on the freedom of religion guaranteed by the First Amendment. The Free Exercise Clause in the First Amendment grants all Americans the freedom to practice their faith, but these laws are an attempt to turn our First Amendment rights upside down, and they must be rejected. If our representatives in Washington fail to listen to the voice of the people, we will need to do two things. First, contact the White House and call on the president to veto any and all hate-crimes legislation. And, second, make sure we know where our congressmen and senators stand on these issues. If they stand with the homosexual lobby, we need to use our votes to find good replacements and send them all home.

THE ASSAULT ON RELIGION

Unfortunately, homosexuals aren't the only ones trying to silence the church today. The assault on the Christian faith is a central feature of the Left's efforts to transform American culture by removing every obstacle to their desired objective, which is powerful central government headed by social liberals. What the First Amendment actually says is, "Congress shall make no law respecting an establishment of religion, or prohibiting the free exercise thereof." It is such a vital part of the laws of this nation that the Founders insisted it must be part of the Constitution. It is also why I put it at the beginning of this book.

What this means is that government is prohibited from setting up a state religion, like that of England or Saudi Arabia, and government may not interfere with the practice of religion—meaning any religion freely chosen. Yet, even though the language is perfectly clear, the courts have actually used this clause to remove religion from schoolrooms, government buildings, public property, football games, graduation ceremonies, and many other places, all in the name of protecting us from what the liberals see as the corrupting values of the Christian faith.

Groups like the ACLU, People for the American Way, Citizens United for the Separation of Church and State, and even the Southern Poverty Law Center, which was such a stalwart defender of authentic civil rights a generation ago, have done their best to make God unconstitutional. Over the last few years, I have written extensively about the assault on religion and the problems created by government's encroachment on religious liberties. But I have been astonished that so few believers seem to grasp the fact that we are engaged in a power struggle with the forces of darkness, who would gladly take our religious liberties away.

What we are dealing with today is nothing short of an all-out assault on the Christian faith, and it is coming from all corners of the secular world. Homosexuals are leading the way, but they are joined by academics, the media, the unions, and many other Democratic strongholds. As I said earlier in this chapter, the war is being waged in the legislatures, schools, and boardrooms of America, and perhaps most of all in the print and broadcast media, where so many of our leading journalists share the views and values of the political Left.

In the spring of 2007, we encountered one more attempt by the Left to force hate crimes laws down our throats when the Democrat leadership in Congress were able to move H.R. 1592 from subcommittee to law in less than three weeks. Many Christians were not aware as the law was being rushed through Congress and passed in early May. Congressional staffers refused to talk to us about the legislation and resorted to calling the major Christian ministries who had alerted our supporters to what was happening "alarmists" and "liars." Among the groups they attacked were Concerned Women for America, Traditional Values Coalition, Family Research Council, Focus on the Family, the High Impact Leadership Coalition, and a host of others.

This bill was nothing short of a "thought-crimes" law designed to silence traditional Judeo-Christian beliefs about the sin of homosexuality and the dangers it represents to civilized society. Although similar laws of this kind are on the books in countries with a well-documented anti-Christian bias, the citizens of this country have been told that we have nothing to fear. But people are beginning to discover how it really works.

In Philadelphia in 2004, as just one example, a Christian group asked for and received permission to gather peacefully at a gay-pride event. Without confrontation or agitation of any kind, they planned to hand out literature and speak to anyone interested about the Christian view of homosexuality. But the moment they showed up, a homosexual hit squad descended on them en masse, blocked their view, shouted profanities, and even called the police to cart them away, which Philadelphia's finest obligingly did. In the melee that followed, a seventy-five-year-old grandmother of three was arrested, jailed, and charged under state hate crimes law for attempting to share the gospel of Jesus Christ.[8]

Ironically, during the rally, none of the homosexual activists were hurt, wounded, or even touched. As often happens at these events, there was shockingly lewd behavior, public nudity, and types of exhibitionism that defy description. But the public officials of Philadelphia sent a loud, clear message to the world: "Gays can protest, intimidate, and harass anyone they wish. But Christians had better not speak, or they'll be thrown in jail."

THE FAIRNESS DOCTRINE

If standing on a public sidewalk and speaking to passersby is ruled a crime, we have to wonder what's next. The answer may well be the return of an antiquated and currently defunct regulation applied by the Federal Communications Commission, known as "the fairness doctrine." Different versions of the fairness doctrine have been around since 1949, when it was used by conservatives to challenge some of the tirades of anarchists and other pro-Soviet agitators on radio broadcasts. The policy required broadcast licensees to present controversial issues in an equal and balanced manner. On the surface, that sounds fine. In the best of all worlds it could mean that the little guy would have a chance to be heard. But the motivation behind such policies today is to silence certain kinds of opinion and to have a chilling effect on free speech.

Ironically, it was the liberal Chief Justice Warren Burger who spoke most forcefully against the unfairness of the fairness doctrine. In the Court's unanimous opinion in the case of *Miami Herald Publishing Co. v. Tornillo* (1974), he wrote, "Government-enforced right of access inescapably dampens the vigor and limits the variety of public debate."[9] The Court's opinion didn't resolve the issue, however. Debate continued for many years without resolution until June 1987, when a Democratic Congress passed S. 742, making the Fairness Doctrine a permanent reality. Fortunately, President Ronald Reagan vetoed the bill, and another attempt to ram it through in 1991 was vetoed by President George H. W. Bush.

In today's politically charged environment, the Fairness Doctrine would no doubt be used to mute the voice of the Christian and conservative talk shows that are having such a big impact on the culture. Conservatives would not be allowed to present a biblical or moral viewpoint without censorship. On the other hand, liberal programs that have been utterly unable to attract an audience would be given an "unfair" advantage. This kind of legislation, if passed, would make it possible for anti-Christian activists to get a free ride on powerful Christian and conservative networks that are the only alternatives to the liberal spin of the secular media.

So far, supporters of the fairness doctrine have been out-foxed, but they will be back, and it will be important for conservatives and principled moderates to let their voices be heard. We are accustomed to attacks from the Left, and we know that we will be on the front lines whenever certain individuals bring forth new and provocative legislation. But now and then we are hit by a curve ball from our own side of the field, and that happened in November 2007 when Republican Senator Chuck Grassley, the ranking member of the Senate Finance Committee, sent letters to six large media ministries demanding disclosure of the financial procedures of their ministries.

In comments about the action reported in the *New York Times*, Grassley said he had questions about compensation, housing allowances, checking and savings accounts, cars, airplanes, and overseas trips made by these ministries, and they were given until December 6, 2007, to respond. Most of these ministers are proponents of the "prosperity gospel," as the *Times* expressed it, which teaches that God rewards those who open their hearts and their wallets. In a subsequent telephone interview, Grassley said, "Jesus comes into the city on a simple mule, and you got people today expanding his gospel in corporate jets. Somebody ought to raise questions about, *Is it right or wrong?*"[10]

FREEDOM HELD HOSTAGE

The ministries being investigated include Creflo and Taffi Dollar of World Changers Church International in College Park, Georgia; Randy and Paula White of Without Walls International Church in Tampa, Florida; Benny Hinn of World Healing Center Church, based in Grapevine, Texas; David and Joyce Meyer of Joyce Meyer Ministries in Fenton, Missouri; Bishop Eddie Long of New Birth Missionary Baptist Church in Lithonia, Georgia; and Kenneth and Gloria Copeland of Kenneth Copeland Ministries in Newark, Texas.[11]

Mr. Grassley's letter said that since these ministries are tax exempt, all contributions must be used for the "tax-exempt purposes of the organizations."[12] If any donations are diverted for the individuals' personal use, it could result in a violation of the federal tax code. He also said that he was simply following up on the concerns of his constituents, but if he doesn't like what he finds out, he could be in a position to shut those ministries down—a statement that ought to raise a red flag for every Christian.

Grassley's concerns may be legitimate, or they may not. They may simply be one more manifestation of the degree to which anti-Christian forces in this country have co-opted the courts, law enforcement, and the legislatures to do their dirty work. Most ministries broadcasting on radio or television these days are evangelical and conservative in their views. Is the senator's action, even though well intentioned, merely another way to silence this important group and force them to back away from speaking out on important social issues? It is something we ought to think about, and it is an area where Christians need to be especially vigilant.

It is striking that the most dangerous attacks on religious freedom are not happening on foreign soil. They are not occurring as a result of terrorists, armed gunmen, or other extremists. They take place daily on national television or in the pages of the mainstream media, and sometimes on the floor of the United States Senate, in front of thousands of witnesses. Religious freedom and freedom of speech are being attacked in the name of misguided compassion for types who have no regard for the history or the moral values of the American people.

One such attack appeared in the guise of Senate bill 1105, referred to by supporters as the "Matthew Shepard Act." Even though it was actually a "hate crimes" bill, it was introduced on the Senate floor as an amendment to the Defense Authorization Bill, which involves funding for the war in Iraq. In case you are wondering what hate crimes have to do with the war in Iraq, the answer is simple. Absolutely nothing!

This move was an example of politics at its worst. The hate crimes bill never went through the Senate subcommittee for discussion or mark-up. Senators were not allowed to discuss the merits of the bill, and the normal process of legislation was entirely circumvented. Senator Ted Kennedy led the effort to pass this bill despite the opposition of millions of Americans. In personal meetings my staff and I held with members of the Senate Judiciary Committee, they admitted that they had received hundreds of calls from outraged citizens. But that didn't stop them; nothing could dissuade the Kennedy contingent.

How can any political party justify changing Senate rules in such a manner? Everyone knows that President Bush had been struggling to get budget authorization for the war. But Ted Kennedy and his cohorts decided to dangle a carrot in front of the president. If he wanted to fund the troops in Iraq, he would have to sign a hate crimes bill, which Kennedy had been trying to shove through Congress for decades.

If the president refused to sign, Kennedy threatened, American soldiers would be left without vital supplies. But, by a stroke of providence, the Lord intervened and made a way where there seemed to be no way. As it turned out, the High Impact Leadership Coalition, which I lead, had just placed a full-page ad in the national newspaper *USA Today* on the same day the bill was brought to the Senate floor. The banner headline read, "Don't Muzzle Our Pulpits!" Thirty-six nationally known black ministers from all over America took a bold stand for the Constitution and the Bible by signing their names to that ad.

The ad read in part, "Christian clergymen and people of faith are making a stand today for religious liberty. We oppose S. 1105, the so-called 'hate crimes' bill. Similar laws at the state level and in other countries have already been used to muzzle the church. Labeling politically incorrect views as 'hate' will have a chilling effect on the free speech and religious liberty of our churches and of our members."

Subsequently, that bill was sent back to the Judiciary Committee for reconsideration and hasn't been heard from since. I felt that was a great victory. But rest assured, the issue isn't dead. This is exactly the kind of subversive attack on our freedom of conscience that we have come to expect from the Left. But it is also a huge motivation for this new and growing coalition of black and white evangelicals. And we are not going away.

■ ■ ■ ■

CHAPTER EIGHT

The Health-Care Conundrum

MY WIFE AND I SAT IN THE OFFICE OF A WORLD-FAMOUS surgeon at one of the nation's most prestigious hospitals. As we stared into the face of this bright young physician, we felt inspired and hopeful. The doctor exuded confidence despite the fact that he told us that the type of cancer I was fighting was especially deadly. On average only 15 percent of patients who follow traditional surgical approaches lived more than five years after surgery. His institution, the world-famous Johns Hopkins University Hospital, had developed a special treatment protocol that was years ahead of most domestic hospitals, and their techniques promised to quadruple my survival prospects.

This treatment required massive doses of chemotherapy, radiation, multiple surgeries, and postsurgical chemo. After conferring with our doctors, we decided to go with the Johns Hopkins approach. The drive to the hospital in Baltimore was a great deal farther than other local hospitals, but we made the commitment because of the caliber of treatment we knew we would receive there.

The biggest shock of the entire process came when we received a large bill for the first minor preparatory surgical treatment— insertion of a special feeding tube and a rare twenty-four-hour chemo-delivery system. These first chemo treatments were identified as "experimental" by the insurance company, and when I racked up a bill of nearly ten thousand dollars in less than two weeks for the preliminary procedures, I wasn't sure whether I could afford to get well or not. Needless to say, there was a constant tug-of-war between the insurance company and me for a while.

The insurance company told me they preferred to use local doctors and local tests. Hopkins, seemingly impervious to the insurance company's complaints, assigned a team of five specialists to manage my case because of several complications I experienced in the course of treatment. Eventually the insurance company paid for all my tests, treatments, and procedures, but it was a struggle I surely didn't need to deal with at that time. The fact that I had cheated death on two separate occasions prior to undergoing major surgery was the defining factor of the treatment protocol I was given.

Today, I am happy to report I have been assured that I am cancer free. I am glad I worked with the physicians at Johns Hopkins Hospital. I am convinced their superior care has contributed to my survival. But the cost of this new lease on life was approximately one hundred thousand dollars in unexpected personal expenses, beyond the cost of more traditional treatments. These numbers don't include personal income loss due to illness. Was it worth the price? You better believe it was, and I am thankful to be alive.

I think everyone in this country is aware that the state of health care is an ongoing concern for many people, and the high cost of health insurance is a hot-button issue in today's political environment. Some of the proposals I have heard for dealing with the problems seem to make good sense, but I have also heard a lot of demagoguery from politicians and pundits about the need for taxpayer-funded nationalized health care, and that gives me pause.

STATE-RUN HEALTH CARE

Recently, a lady at my health club stopped me to inquire about my doctors and the treatment I was receiving. Her father, who lives in England under universal health care, has the same type of cancer but was essentially sent home to die. She is attempting to get my doctor to consult with his physicians overseas, but I understand that may be very difficult because of the strict regulations imposed by the British National Health Service.

The main complaints I have heard from people who live in Britain, Canada, and other places where state-run health care has been implemented is that it takes so long to get an appointment to see a physician, to be admitted for treatment, and especially to receive the specialized treatments that are often required for serious illnesses, including heart disease, cancer, and other potentially fatal conditions. Because everything from the price of medicine to the salaries paid to doctors and nurses are regulated by the government, patients routinely become the victims of cost-cutting measures that are not in their best interest.

In June of 2001, it was reported that more than 1,038,000 British citizens were on the hospital waiting lists, uncertain if and when they would ever see a doctor. Nearly 76,000 of those had been on the list for more than three months, and some had been waiting for as long as eighteen months. Many of these people had long-term and potentially fatal diseases, which makes me wonder what might have happened to someone in my condition if nationalized health care were the only option.

But these are not new problems for those who live in Britain and other nations of the European Union. Thousands of British and Canadian doctors have emigrated to the United States over the past two decades because of restrictions on what they can and cannot prescribe, as well as the lower income potential under nationalized health care. A secondary result of crowding and the departures of many of the best-trained physicians has been a lowering of the requirements for medical professionals. In order to meet the growing need for physicians, the British government has had to recruit thousands of foreign-trained doctors to practice in that country.

The controversial filmmaker Michael Moore boasted about England's National Health Service (NHS) in his documentary

Sicko. But you have to wonder what there is to boast about when record numbers of British citizens, identified as "health tourists," feel they have to travel abroad for better and faster treatment. Most of these people are paying for treatment out of their own pockets. According to a report in the *London Sunday Telegraph,* more than seventy thousand Britons traveled abroad for medical treatment in 2007 alone. The NHS estimated that as many as two hundred thousand will choose to leave the UK for treatment by the end of the decade.[1]

Many of these patients are traveling as far as India for surgery, and countries such as Hungary, Turkey, Germany, Malaysia, Poland, and Spain are common destinations for "health tourists." The Web site "Treatment Abroad" reports that Britons have traveled to 112 foreign hospitals in 48 countries to find safe, affordable care. And because of crowding, inattentive health-care providers, and generally lax conditions in many of Britain's hospitals and clinics, there has been a shocking rise in infections by the superbug *Clostridium difficile.* The *Telegraph* article indicates that there has been a 500 percent increase in diagnosed cases of this deadly staphlike infection in just the last 10 years. There were 55,000 such cases reported in 2006.

But perhaps the most eye-opening comment was that of Katherine Murphy of the Patients' Association in London, who said, "People are simply frightened of going to NHS hospitals, so I am not surprised the numbers going abroad are increasing so rapidly. My fear is that most people can't afford to have private treatment—whether in this country or abroad." Yet, in a nationwide survey on this issue, almost all of those who traveled abroad for treatment said they would do it again if the need should ever arise. Who could blame them?

MAKING HEALTH CARE AFFORDABLE

I am convinced that Americans have the finest doctors and best hospitals in the world. Our national conundrum is how to help each individual get the care they need. Unfortunately, many Americans have too few treatment options available to them. Further, a large number of Americans aren't covered at all. I have yet to see the program that answers all these questions, but I am encouraged by the direction that some of our opinion leaders seem to be going.

Recently, Senator Sam Brownback said, "Our healthcare system will thrive with increased consumer choice, consumer control, and real competition. I believe it's important that we have price transparency within our healthcare system. This offers consumers, who are either enrolled in high deductible health plans or who pay out-of-pocket, the ability to shop around for the best prices and plan for health care expenditures."[2]

I am glad to know that some of our elected officials are beginning to think more creatively about how to maintain the high quality of care while reducing costs and expanding the safety net for those who simply cannot afford the high cost of private health insurance. Former New York Mayor Rudy Giuliani's Web site addressed this issue as well, saying, "America is at a crossroads when it comes to our health care. All Americans want to increase the quality, affordability, and portability of health care....I believe we can reduce costs and improve the quality of care by increasing competition. We can do it through tax cuts, not tax hikes. We can do it by empowering patients and their doctors, not government bureaucrats. That's the American way to reform health care."[3]

Another candidate, former Arkansas Governor Mike Huckabee, addressed the high cost of health care as well, saying, "Spending is now about $2 trillion a year, which is close to $7,000 for each one of us. It consumes about 17 percent of our gross domestic product, easily surpassing the few European nations where spending is close to 10 percent and far higher than any other country in the world. If we reduced our out-of-control health-care costs from 17 percent to 11 percent, we would save $700 billion a year, which is about twice our annual national deficit."[4] Cost really does seem to be the biggest concern, and these suggestions make a lot of sense to me.

We know the product is good, but a lot of Americans simply can't afford it. So what do we do? For one thing, the tax code needs to be reformed so that Americans without private health coverage can deduct the cost of medicines and treatments. Tax credits may be the best answer for middle-income families, and tax rebates would be a better option for those at the lower end of the economic ladder, whenever legitimate need is established. I have also read several reports dealing with the need to accelerate the pace of drug evaluations and approvals by the Food and Drug Administration to insure that newly discovered products can get to those who need them sooner, and this also needs to be discussed.

HELPING AFRICAN AMERICANS

According to the Web site BlackHealthCare.com, the state of health for African Americans today is precarious. The incidence of diabetes among African Americans is about 70 percent higher than it is for whites. The infant mortality rate is twice as high for African Americans as for whites, and the five-year survival rate for cancer among African Americans diagnosed between 1986–1992 is about 44 percent, compared to 59 percent for whites.

The HIV/AIDS epidemic, which was first reported in this country in 1981, is nothing short of a global crisis. The percentage of blacks diagnosed with one of these conditions is greatly disproportionate to the infection rate in the general population. The HIV virus, which is the first stage of full-blown AIDS, progressively destroys the body's ability to fight infections and certain cancers by killing or damaging the cells of the immune system. Men and women diagnosed with HIV/AIDS become vulnerable to opportunistic infections caused by microbes that normally wouldn't cause illness in healthy people, but which can lead to life-threatening diseases for those whose immune systems are compromised.

According to the Centers for Disease Control and Prevention (CDC), more than 600,000 cases of AIDS have been reported in the United States since 1981, and as many as 900,000 Americans may be infected with HIV. The epidemic is growing fastest in the minority population and has been identified as one of the leading killers of African American males. The prevalence of AIDS is six times higher in African Americans and three times higher among Hispanics than among whites.[5]

According to the 2000 national census figures, African Americans make up about 12.9 percent of the U.S. population—or about 36.4 million individuals. Even though blacks are a relatively small segment of the population, the National Center for Minority Health and Health Disparities, a division of the National Institutes of Health, reports that blacks in general have a higher rate of occurrence, a higher death rate, and a larger number of serious health conditions than whites or other minority populations in the this country.[6]

For many health conditions, non-Hispanic blacks have greater rates of disease, injury, death, and disability. The top three causes of death, and seven of the ten leading causes of death, are the same for blacks and whites; however, the morbidity and mortality rates for these diseases and injuries are greater among blacks than whites. In addition, three of the ten leading causes of death for non-Hispanic blacks are not among the leading causes of death for non-Hispanic whites—including homicide, HIV disease, and septicemia.[7]

According to CDC records from 2002, which are the most recent data for these issues, cancer is the second leading cause of death for both blacks and whites. However, in 2001 the age-adjusted incidence per 100,000 population was substantially higher for black females than for white females for certain cancers, including colon/rectal (54.0 versus 43.3), pancreatic (13.0 versus 8.9), and stomach cancers (9.0 versus 4.5). Among males, the age-adjusted incidence was higher for black males than for white males for certain cancers, including prostate (251.3 versus 167.8), lung/bronchus (108.2 versus 72.8), colon/rectal (68.3 versus 58.9), and stomach cancers (16.3 versus 10.0).

In addition, 2002 statistics show that blacks had substantially higher proportions of certain lifestyle-related health indicators than non-Hispanic whites, including new cases of gonorrhea (742 versus 31 per 100,000 population); deaths from homicide (21.6 versus 2.8); persons aged six to nineteen years who were overweight or obese (22 percent versus 12 percent); and adults who were obese (40 percent versus 29 percent).[8]

PAYING FOR TREATMENT

The statistics may seem cold and impersonal, but every one of them represents human lives that are being threatened or lost due to the risks and general social conditions within our communities. If we start to believe that we are invulnerable, or if we take too many risks with our health, there will be a price to pay. In the eyes of God, every life is precious, from cradle to grave. Scripture tells us that God is "not willing that any should perish, but that all should come to repentance" (2 Pet. 3:9). In addition, we have the assurance that "length of days, and long life, and peace" are what God desires for us (Prov. 3:2). However, it is our responsibility to live in ways that will improve our chances for a long and healthy life.

It is no real surprise that African Americans lag behind whites and other minority groups in the percentage of individuals covered by health-care insurance. Because of the income differential between the races, fewer black families can afford insurance policies that are not funded primarily by their employers. Nationally, about 56 percent of African Americans have private health insurance coverage, and Medicaid covers about 21 percent. Still, nearly a quarter of African Americans (23 percent) are uninsured. According to researchers at the Kaiser Family Foundation, the uninsured rate for African Americans is more than one and a half times the rate for whites, largely because of gaps in employer-based coverage.[9]

Although over 80 percent of African Americans are in working families, employer-sponsored health insurance among African Americans remains substantially lower than that of whites (53 percent vs. 73 percent). This is somewhat surprising in today's economy, which has improved access to job-based health benefits for most American workers. Still the fact remains that African Americans are three times as likely as whites to live in poverty, and half of all African Americans have family incomes less than 200 percent of the poverty level. Lower family income means a much lower likelihood of having employer-based health coverage.[10]

The Kaiser report, produced in collaboration with the UCLA Center for Health Policy Research, shows that African Americans are less likely to have job-based coverage at all income levels than whites. This is apparently true even though African Americans are more likely than other groups to work in large businesses that typically offer health benefits. Furthermore, African Americans are substantially less likely than whites to receive job-based coverage across all firm sizes and industries.

Medicaid provides an important safety net for one in five African Americans, underscoring the role that Medicaid plays for low-income families with children. Medicaid covers half of African Americans with incomes below poverty and 17 percent of those between 100 and 199 percent of poverty. So this is an important safety net for many of our people. However, 30 percent of African Americans below 200 percent of poverty remain uninsured.[11]

In his 2007 State of the Union address, President Bush recognized these disparities in health coverage and pledged to work with Congress to find new options and increase government support for those least able to afford private coverage. In that speech, he said, "A future of hope and opportunity requires that all our citizens have affordable and available health care. When it comes to health care, government has an obligation to care for the elderly, the disabled, and poor children. And we will meet those responsibilities. For all other Americans, private health insurance is the best way to meet their needs. But many Americans cannot afford a health insurance policy."[12]

Over the next few minutes of his address, President Bush sketched the outlines of his proposal to offer a standard tax deduction for those with health insurance similar to the deduction currently offered for families with dependent children. He said the IRS Code could be revised so that families with health insurance would pay no income or payroll taxes on the first $15,000 of income. Unmarried persons with health insurance would have a similar deduction on $7,500 of income. If implemented, that could provide tax relief for approximately 100 million Americans.

AFFORDABLE ALTERNATIVES

For those who purchase private health insurance, the proposal would offer a tax savings of $60,000 for a family of four. For the millions of Americans who have no health insurance, he said, these tax deductions would help put private health insurance within reach of many more. The IRS is not the most flexible bureaucracy in town, but changing the tax code, Bush said, is a "vital and necessary step to making health care affordable for more Americans."[13] I agree; that is an important first step.

The president also suggested that the federal government ought to be helping states that are coming up with innovative new ways to cover the uninsured. States that make basic health insurance available to their citizens, he said, would receive federal funds to help cover the most needy. A series of Affordable Choices Grants would be made available through the Office of Health and Human Services, from existing federal funds. The purpose of these measures would be to give the governors of all fifty states more money and more flexibility in providing coverage for those who need it most.

There has been a lot of debate about the president's proposals for Health Savings Accounts (HSAs), which would involve a private savings account similar to an IRA, with matching funds to be available at time of need. The president discussed this proposal as well and then spoke about the need to reduce costs and medical errors, to increase price transparency so that patients will be able to see exactly what they are paying for, and to put limits on frivolous lawsuits that drive up the cost of medical care and medications.

Another initiative that ignited flames of controversy in 2007 was proposed legislation for a bill titled "State Children's Health Insurance Program" (SCHIP). Lawmakers came up with this program to provide private health coverage for children whose parents earned too much money to qualify for Medicaid but not enough to afford private health coverage. However, in the sausage-making process, Congress expanded the measure to provide coverage to families earning up to 300 percent of the federal poverty level (or about $60,000 for a family of four) and "children" up to twenty-five years of age. President Bush called it "welfare for middle-class households" and vetoed the bill in its current form, but he encouraged Congress to restore the legislation to its original form.[14]

In published remarks after the veto, the president said, "Put poor children first. I urge Republicans and Democrats in Congress to support a bill that moves adults off this children's program—and covers children who do not qualify for Medicaid, but whose families are struggling." The goal, he said, "should be to move children who have no health insurance to private coverage, not to move children who already have private health insurance to government coverage."[15]

Democrats accused Bush of "moving the goal posts," and they refused to meet with his designated health-care specialists to negotiate a better version of the bill that would serve poor kids first. One independent analyst who studied the bill pointed out that provisions of the vetoed bill would have paid for the full cost of health insurance for "children" up to age twenty-eight, with household incomes up to $80,000. That was never the purpose of the legislation, and I think it was a serious political miscalculation by the Democrats. Nevertheless, the Democratic leaders in the House made a few minor adjustments to the bill and passed it again.

BLACK GENOCIDE

There is no doubt that wrangling of this kind will continue indefinitely so long as the nation remains so intensely divided between Left and Right. Meanwhile, millions of Americans are suffering, and social pathologies in our neighborhoods are out of control. One of the most serious concerns is the shocking abortion rate in African American neighborhoods. I have called it a form of "black genocide," and the numbers of babies aborted in the black community are truly heartbreaking. The Left doesn't see this as a major problem. Maybe they are in denial about the number of kids that are aborted each year. Something has to be done.

A couple of years ago I did a lot of research on this. What I found is that seven in ten black children today are born out of wedlock.[16] In addition, the black abortion rate is very high. When you see the statistics on the number of teenage pregnancies, you have to wonder: Are a lot of these black abortions being sought by adult women who already have children and are just trying to raise the ones they have? Are they trying to raise kids without a father in the house? Or are they just troubled girls trying to solve a problem? Whatever the cause, the so-called "easy solution" taken by many black women today is terribly wrong.

Between 1882 and 1968, approximately 3,446 blacks were lynched in the United States. That is a number that horrifies most people, and it is shocking. But according to statistics from the Life Education And Resource Network (LEARN) on the Internet, that number is surpassed in less than three days by the abortion of black children in this country. As many as 1,452 African American babies are killed each day in America. Since 1973, more than 13 million children have been murdered and their mothers victimized by the abortion industry.[17]

Martin Luther King Jr. wrote, "They [the early church] brought an end to such ancient evils as infanticide."[18] I think we have a pretty good idea what Dr. King would say about the tragedy of abortion. In the name of "a woman's right to choose," we have gone from infanticide to genocide. We have done it by an edict of the Court, and a lot of African Americans have been convinced that this is a perfectly normal thing to do. What a fraud!

Several years ago, when Jesse Jackson still cared about such things, he said, "Those advocates of taking life prior to birth do not call it killing or murder, they call it abortion. They further never talk about aborting a baby because that would imply something human. Rather they talk about aborting the *fetus*. Fetus sounds less than human and therefore abortion can be justified."[19] As African American pro-life advocates at the LEARN Web site expressed it, "Jackson's massive flip-flop on the abortion issue is further proof that his political future is far more important to him than are his principles."[20]

The real tragedy is that one-third of all abortions in this country today are performed on black women, while the abortion industry rakes in more than four billion dollars from the black community. What could be more horrible than black genocide for profit?

From the book I wrote with George Barna, we know that 47 percent of African Americans claim to be born-again Christians.[21] There actually may be more than that, but the research model excluded those who didn't meet certain criteria or who claimed to be Christians but didn't understand certain basic doctrines of the faith. The point is that this is statistically higher than the number of white evangelicals who identify themselves as Christians.

If there are that many people who truly understand the moral values of the Christian faith, why are we seeing such casual disregard for human life? How can anyone dare to call himself or herself a follower of Jesus Christ when they think so little of destroying innocent life in the womb? How is that living out our faith? The problem in our lifestyle and personal habits is all about sex and sexuality. This is true to some degree for both blacks and whites, but the hypersexualized culture our young people are exposed to, day in and day out, is causing serious problems in the black community. Abortion is one of the worst.

A TIME FOR TRANSFORMATION

As I have said several times in these pages, the family safety net is broken, and it has to be fixed. There is a dangerous lack of two-parent families, which just makes the whole situation worse. There is a history of underachievement, which is so pervasive that we have young people in our schools who call high achievement "acting white."

At some point, we have to step up to the plate. Whatever you think about abortion as a legal option for women, it is always a tragedy. In every case, there are at least two victims: the one who dies and the one who will be wounded for life. Even beyond that, the entire community suffers. How many future doctors, lawyers, teachers, coaches, or great athletes will never have a chance to achieve their success in life because they were murdered in the womb? How many women will cry themselves to sleep every night because of the agony and guilt they feel?

Several years ago when organizations like Planned Parenthood were spreading their tentacles across the nation, setting up abortion mills in practically every city and town, a group of caring Christians started the first crisis pregnancy centers to counsel women considering an abortion, telling them about the many options that were available to them and their unborn child. Today there are more than 2,300 of these centers across the country; yet, until recently, very few of them happened to be in inner-city neighborhoods where the abortion rate is highest.

However, the two largest networks of crisis pregnancy centers in North America—Care Net and Heartbeat International—have launched new initiatives to change that. They are doing it in the most surprising way, through an antiabortion movement led mostly by white Republicans who are interacting on a one-on-one basis with women in overwhelmingly Democratic black communities.

In one article I read about this new program, Lillie Epps, who is the only black member of Care Net's senior staff and director of its Urban Initiative, said the work has been difficult. The biggest challenge has been to educate black leaders as to what is really going on and then talking with them about how the abortion rate is affecting their community without being offensive or appearing to have a political agenda. She also said it is an important and timely challenge that she is more than happy to accept.[22]

In Washington DC, which has one of the highest abortion rates in the country, there is now a Care Net affiliate in the downtown area, the Capitol Hill Crisis Pregnancy Center, as well as a teen center, called The House DC, in the tough Anacostia neighborhood. During the school year, the article reported, volunteers from the Capitol Hill Center make the short drive over to The House to counsel young women from nearby Anacostia High School who are either pregnant or at risk of getting caught up in the crucible of abortion.

This is a fascinating story, because it shows how faith can bring black and white Christians together to make a real difference. The teen center's black leadership and the whites who run the pregnancy center are born-again Christians. One man who is making a big difference is the cofounder of The House, former professional football player Steve Fitzhugh, who is also an active member of the Fellowship of Christian Athletes. Steve said that he has mentored boys who were later killed in gang shootings and girls as young as twelve who made the decision to carry their pregnancies to term. Steve is a caring mentor, and that is what really makes the difference.

ECONOMIC CONSIDERATIONS

Personal involvement is essential, but I believe there is another dimension to the health-care issue, and this is something that Tavis Smiley dealt with in his book, which I discussed briefly in chapter 4. That is, in some of our poorer communities, it is much harder to have access to proper nutritional items. Poor neighborhoods generally don't have access to great supermarkets with fresh foods and quality groceries. So we need to talk about urban development, exploring ways to attract supermarkets and stores where people can get wholesome products, such as fresh fruits and vegetables, as well as vitamins, minerals, and other necessary items.

One hopeful sign on the development scene is the improvement in both the job market and the income level of African Americans over the last several years. This is an important factor in determining whether or not new businesses will be willing to relocate to our inner-city neighborhoods.

The August 2007 announcement from the Census Bureau that the number of families living in poverty declined from 12.6 percent in 2005 to 12.3 percent in calendar year 2006 was good news. At the same time, median household income increased to $48,200. An Associated Press report in the pages of the *Washington Post* suggested, however, that the good news is tempered by recent concerns in the housing market over defaults in home loans and an increase in the number of Americans without health insurance—up from 44.8 million in 2005 to 47 million in 2006. But higher incomes for blacks is always good news.[23]

Douglas Besharov, a scholar at the American Enterprise Institute, told the *Post* reporters he thought that, even with the downturns in a couple of areas, there was a lot of good news in the new census numbers. "We're looking at a situation where unemployment was down, and it was down for single mothers, who make up a substantial portion of the people in poverty. We need a good economy," he said. "That's not all we need, but we shouldn't complain when it helps lower poverty."

Predictably, not everyone was happy about the good news. Representative Charles Rangel of New York, the Democratic chairman of the House Ways and Means Committee, complained, "Too many Americans find themselves still stuck in the deep hole dug by economic policies favoring the wealthy. Income remains lower than it was six years ago, poverty is higher, and the number of Americans without health insurance continues to grow."

A more realistic assessment of these issues can be found in a study by Robert Rector of the Heritage Foundation, who made a detailed analysis of poverty in the United States. For a quarter of a century prior to welfare reform, Rector says, the poverty rate for black children in this country was frozen at around 42 percent. Since welfare reform in 1996, that figure dropped to about 30 percent in 2001—the lowest in history. In 2003, the poverty rate for black children rose but was still modest, at 33.6 percent. Despite changes in the economy since that time, nearly a million black children have been lifted out of poverty over the past twelve years.[24]

While the newest Census Bureau data indicate an increase in the number of persons without health insurance, their count may be unreliable. Rector points out that census figures are always higher regarding the "uninsured" than the totals given by other government surveys, such as the Survey of Income and Program Participation and the Medical Expenditure Panel Survey. He believes this is because of the undercount in the number of Medicaid enrollments. In 2003, 53 million Americans were enrolled in Medicaid but the census only reported 35.6 million. Medicaid enrollments have expanded dramatically since that time, but the Census Bureau figures still don't reflect the increase.

A Second Look at Poverty

I sometimes get the impression from these debates that poverty is whatever the politicians want it to be. Each administration boasts that they have reduced poverty and the other party has made it worse. This was certainly true for both the Clinton and Bush administrations. But there are actual measures of poverty, and when you find out what poverty looks like in America, you get a very different impression of what we need to do to fix it.

For most people, the word *poverty* means rock-bottom destitution, homelessness, an inability to feed your family, dirty clothes, junk cars, and standing on the street corner begging for quarters. Except for homeless people and chronic substance abusers who end up in inner-city shelters, very few Americans even get close to that level of poverty. It is true, some people are on hard times in some of our urban areas, but most of those labeled as "poor" in this country live in conditions that would be considered well-to-do in most other countries.

For example, 46 percent of all poor households own their own homes. The average home owned by persons classified as "poor" by Census Bureau reports is a three-bedroom house with one and a half baths, a garage, and a porch or patio.[25] Today fully 76 percent of poor households have air conditioning. Thirty years ago, just 36 percent of the entire United States population had air conditioning. Also, only 6 percent of poor households are overcrowded. More than two-thirds of all such households have more than two rooms per person.

The average poor American has more living space than the average individual living in Paris, London, Vienna, Athens, and other cities throughout Europe. Nearly three-fourths of poor households in this country own a car; 30 percent own two or more cars. Ninety-seven percent of poor households have a color television. Over half own two or more color televisions. Seventy-eight percent of America's poor own a VCR or DVD player; 62 percent have cable or satellite TV reception. Seventy-three percent own microwave ovens, more than half have a stereo, and one-third have an automatic dishwasher.

Rector points out that, as a group, America's poor are far from being chronically undernourished. The average consumption of protein, vitamins, and minerals is virtually the same for poor and middle-class children and, in most cases, is above the recommended norms. Poor children consume more meat than higher-income children and have average protein intakes that are 100 percent above the recommended levels. Most poor children in America are, in fact, supernourished and grow up to be, on average, an inch taller and ten pounds heavier, as this researcher puts it, "than the GIs who stormed the beaches of Normandy in World War II."

For the most part, as figures from the Census Bureau's 2004 Population Survey reveal, long-term poverty today is mostly self-inflicted. George Mason University economist Walter Williams offers this challenging analogy. There is one segment of the black population, he says, that suffers only a 9.9 percent poverty rate, and only 13.7 percent of their under-five-year-olds are identified as "poor." Another segment, however, suffers from a 39.5 percent poverty rate, and 58.1 percent of its under-five-year-olds are "poor."

Among whites, one population segment suffers a 6 percent poverty rate, and only 9.9 percent of its under-five-year-olds are "poor." Another segment of the white population suffers a 26.4 percent poverty rate, and 52 percent of its under-five-year-olds are "poor." Williams asks, "What do you think distinguishes these high and low poverty populations?" The only statistical difference between the black and white populations is marriage. There is far less poverty in married-couple families, where presumably at least one of the spouses is employed. But 85 percent of black children identified by researchers as "poor" live in female-headed households.

A University of Michigan study shows that only 5 percent of those in the bottom fifth of the income distribution in 1975 were still there in 1991. What happened? They moved up to the top three-fifths of the income distribution—meaning that sixteen years later they were in the "middle class or higher" category. Moreover, three out of ten of the lowest income earners in 1975 moved all the way into the top fifth of income earners by 1991. The bottom line, says Dr. Williams, is that the rich *are* getting richer, but the poor are getting richer too.

THE FREE-MARKET OPTION

For generations now, some of our people have been making bad decisions. In addition to the high abortion rate, the high rates of out-of-wedlock childbirth, the number of female-headed households, and the troubling disease statistics I have discussed in this chapter, there is also a high mortality rate. Our people are not very good about getting regular checkups. Too often they won't see a doctor until they are about to drop, and, as we have seen, a fairly large number don't have insurance. So, after examining all these issues, how do we go about fixing them?

The solution offered by Senator Hillary Clinton during her presidential campaign, very much like the one she proposed back in 1994, is essentially a national health service similar to those in Britain, Canada, Sweden, and other socialist nations. This means you pay for health care through your taxes, with a percentage of every dollar you earn, whether or not you ever need to see a doctor. Then you take whatever you are given with no questions asked.

The architects of Senator Clinton's plan insist that patients will be able to choose their own doctors, with some restrictions. As with most of today's health maintenance organizations (HMOs), however, you will not be able to choose your hospital or treatment center. Many times you may not see a doctor at all, and when you do, more than likely you will have to wait until they get around to it. Judging by the English examples I described earlier, that can take awhile. This is one reason why the American people are skeptical of Senator Clinton's proposals.

What needs to happen now is a practical compromise between nationalized health care and our current system. What I would like to see is basically a free-market system with a safety net for those people who don't have the resources to pay for private health care. I have mentioned this a couple of times already, but I think this is the best and most logical plan. The free-market system means that people will be free to shop for their own medical care, which means, in turn, that they are going to be more cautious and not just accept anything that comes along.

People are generally more conservative in their buying decisions when they're spending their own money. Consequently, the system will have to be self-regulating in order to maintain profitability. Since we have the best medical systems in the world, we can generally find a plan that is tailored to our needs. Therefore when programs like the ones I'm describing here become available, we'll also have health-care catalogs, magazines, and medical search engines on the Internet to help us decide which health-care options and which hospitals and treatment centers will be best for our individual needs.

With a system like this, we won't have the problems associated with universal health care, including the long waits, inferior service, higher prices, and other system deficiencies that have been a problem in Canada and Europe. There is room for debate on these issues, of course. As I said earlier, we need to have a new kind of creative thinking and cross-pollination between government, private citizens, physicians, and health-care providers in order to iron out the wrinkles, but if we ever hope to solve the health-care conundrum, it has to happen. That's what I would like to see.

■ ■ ■ ■

CHAPTER NINE

A Tipping Point for Conservatives

WITH MY FOCUS ON PERSONAL INVOLVEMENT AND SOME OF the comments I have made about the failures of big government, some readers of this book may wonder if I believe government can ever help. Government programs, as I said in the previous chapter, are generally costly and seldom successful in what they set out to do, but now and then we see a ray of hope. One such example took place in the summer of 2007, when HUD Secretary Alphonso Jackson and Education Secretary Margaret Spellings sat down with a group of civic leaders at the Civil Rights Museum in Memphis, Tennessee.[1]

The museum was built on the site of the assassination of Dr. Martin Luther King Jr. In fact, the room that Dr. King rented the night before he died is there, and it remains exactly as it was at the time of his death in April 1968. That all happened forty years ago, and I have often wondered if the civil rights movement wasn't mortally wounded in Memphis and bled to death over the next few years.

When Secretary Jackson addressed the guests at the conference in Memphis, he made a remarkable statement. He said, "We are announcing [that] a new civil rights movement begins today." What a striking declaration. Jackson's words weren't aimed at discrediting or upstaging the heroes of America's most effective grassroots social justice movement. Instead, they signaled a desire to complete the work that Dr. King and others had begun. His message was that the best way to create an atmosphere for learning and achievement is to have intact families and stable homes.[2]

This raises the question, what can government do to create stable homes? One answer would be to have more creative housing programs to give incentives to motivated families, to help them develop stronger home lives. The government's HOPE VI program, as Secretary Jackson pointed out, has been used by HUD for more than fifteen years to transform substandard public housing into mixed-income and market-based communities. The "mixed use" concept places needy families and single parents into communities where they can adapt to life in a normal neighborhood that models personal achievement and stability.

When Secretary Spellings spoke, she told the audience in Memphis she is a firm believer in combining the power of accountable public education with a secure home environment. She said that a quality education is the most important first step for community building and made a commitment to fight "the soft bigotry of low expectations" by "strengthening schools and closing the achievement gap." These were important words, and this new initiative may actually do some good if the government does more than just talk about it.

I know that education can be a ticket out of the ghetto; again, my own experience proves that. In elementary school, I had a special bond with two other boys. We did everything together: we played sports, studied, and hung out together. I am sure I was the worst athlete of the bunch, but I could hold my own academically. We all attended the most advanced classes in our all-black urban school. The school was staffed by some of the most committed black teachers I have ever known, and I think we got a reasonably good start.

Of the three of us, however, I was the only one who had a secure home life with a dad who was always present. My father felt that the public schools in my neighborhood would not challenge me enough to reach my potential, so, as I described earlier, he sat me down and told me he had enrolled me in a prestigious private school. There was no minority scholarship program, and this school's tuition ran into thousands of dollars a year. But my parents scraped together the money and believed for the best, and I can honestly say that their decision to invest in education changed the course of my life.

I was exposed to a myriad of things I would never have seen otherwise. My two buddies weren't so fortunate, however. One of them wound up in prison by age eighteen for killing another man in a fight. The other—the fastest sprinter in our school—had to work during his high school years instead of playing sports and ended up driving a city bus in Cincinnati.

At a time when it is too easy to be cynical about the government, I am willing to hold out hope for programs like the ones discussed that day in Memphis. Secretaries Jackson and Spellings may be on the right track—only time will tell. But I'm encouraged by Mr. Jackson's words during a local school visit he made at that time. He said, "We believe that excellence transcends income level....A good education should not be off limits to a family of modest means. Neither should a good home." To that, I say amen.

THE AGONY OF DEFEAT

If the government lives up to its promises, I will be the first to give them a hand. But more often than not big government programs turn out to be big disappointments. It is important for government to take our concerns seriously, but the best solutions for most of our neighborhoods are those that come through cooperative efforts of the people who live there, who understand what is actually at stake, and who often have a pretty good idea of how to fix it. The closer to home a problem is solved, the more satisfying the results will be.

To understand why I believe it is so important for this generation to take responsibility for its own success, it may help to look back briefly at where we have come from. The situation for blacks in this country, from the end of slavery in 1861 to the present, has been mixed. There have been periods of revival and growth countered by longer periods of recession in the black community. Some of it has come from changes within the community, but much of it has been brought about by changes beyond our control.

During the Reconstruction Era there were many blacks holding public office; new communities were being formed, and things were looking up. Then there was a backlash with groups like the Ku Klux Klan unleashing a particularly nasty form of terrorism in the South. When this happened, the amazing beginning for newly freed blacks began to dissipate. By the end of the nineteenth century, there was clearly a regression, and what should have been an upward move became instead a dramatic decline in race relations. This was a time of great struggle and uncertainty for black families.

There was also a large migration from the rural South to the industrial North at this time, along with a general population shift away from the farms to the cities. People were looking for better conditions, but they were fleeing what they considered to be the oppression of the South. For many people, these changes meant that they would have a chance for a better life, but it also meant that the positive momentum they had experienced in the years immediately following the Civil War was gone.

So now you have blacks coming to the North, and they are workers in the industrial machine, as opposed to landowners, farmers, businessmen, politicians, and respected citizens. For many it must have felt like going from one form of slavery to the next. By the 1920s, there were pockets of entrepreneurship and growth in some of the larger cities. The period known today as the Harlem Renaissance was a time when African American poets, writers, and playwrights in New York City began to write about the black experience and to celebrate the journey of our people.

A CREATIVE SURGE

There were periods of creativity both before and after the black exodus began. Many of the works produced by black writers and poets are taught in the schools and universities today. Some, like Langston Hughes, Countee Cullen, and Zora Neale Hurston, are among the greatest writers this country has produced. Later writers such as Richard Wright, James Baldwin, and Ralph Ellison helped to express the hopes, dreams, and fears of black people, as well as the sense of desperation many people felt during those times.

Just when things seemed to be looking up, the stock market crashed in 1929 and the Great Depression brought hunger, misery, and helplessness to many communities. From 1929 to 1940 the entire nation was on life support, and no segment of the population suffered more than African Americans. Where there had been mostly low wages and dirty jobs before the crash, jobs were fewer, dirtier, and much lower paying afterward. President Franklin Roosevelt introduced a series of relief efforts at that time to provide employment and basic necessities for those who were most in need, but it wasn't until the outbreak of World War II that things began to change due to the growth of a wartime economy.

This meant that blacks were suddenly being drafted for military service along with everyone else. For the most part, they served in separate all-black units, but the good news was that for the first time since the Civil War, black soldiers could earn rank based on merit. These soldiers were well fed and learned military discipline. A majority of blacks were assigned to service units as cooks, orderlies, and maintenance workers. Some young men who demonstrated leadership potential were able to go for advanced training as commissioned and noncommissioned officers. The army's 92nd and 93rd Divisions were all-black combat units, and there were several squadrons of black pilots who served in the Army Air Corps in Europe and the Pacific.

Between 1940 and 1945, nearly 900,000 African American soldiers and sailors wore the uniform, and roughly 500,000 saw duty overseas. Under the New Deal, Congress created a national Fair Employment Practices Committee to assist minorities returning to civilian life to find jobs. But when the war ended, discrimination was still a problem, and Jim Crow practices continued in many places in both the North and the South.

Genuine prosperity normally requires generations to achieve. If one generation is able to make a start and lay a foundation, the next generation can begin to add value and build on top of that achievement. That is how society develops. But if that process is thwarted and at every step the foundations of each generation are ripped away, then it will be impossible to advance. This describes how many blacks felt in the years after the war. Every step forward was met with a major setback, and it was in this environment that the civil rights movement was born.

What Martin Luther King Jr. and other black leaders recognized during the 1950s was that there was no mechanism in this country for actually fulfilling the promise of "liberty and justice for all" in the Pledge of Allegiance. Since the early 1950s, Dr. King had been calling attention to the unequal status of blacks. He organized the boycott that ended racially segregated seating on public transportation. The Supreme Court ruled in *Brown v. the Board of Education of Topeka (KS)* (1954) that segregation in public schools was unconstitutional. But it wasn't until nearly ten years later that school officials in Alabama finally began implementing that decision.

EXPLOITATION AND ANARCHY

Racial tensions were at an all-time high in 1963 when four black children were killed by a bomb detonated in a Birmingham church. That incident outraged the entire nation and became a rallying cry that contributed to the passage of the Civil Rights Act of 1964. Then, the following year, Dr. King led the now-famous march from Selma to the state capital at Montgomery, Alabama, to draw attention to the discrimination in voter registration. Subsequently, Congress passed the Voting Rights Act of 1965, which brought many Southern blacks into the political process. This, in turn, helped to modify many of the Jim Crow laws that had plagued blacks not only in the South but also in other parts of the country.

When I was growing up, my parents believed strongly in the importance of a good education, and they insisted that their children make learning a priority. They put us into good schools and helped us along the way because they knew that education is the key to opportunity. I am grateful for their philosophy, but it really makes me sad to hear today's young people saying that studying and making good grades in school is "acting white." I don't know where that attitude comes from, but that kind of thinking is degrading and self-defeating.

What we need in the black community now is a generation of young men and women who want to make something of themselves. Many of the obstacles to social progress have been removed, and there are more opportunities for achievement today than ever before. We need a new set of goals and priorities that will help to establish a black entrepreneurial class. If we don't have people who become engines of progress, financial success, and social empowerment, then we will continue to be handicapped by our status, and our people will continue to be little more than wards of the state. That is definitely not Dr. King's dream for America, and we cannot allow that attitude to continue.

According to some of the research I have seen, a black person with an undergraduate degree is commonly paid about 25 percent less than a white person with a comparable degree. A black person with a master's degree will be paid a few percentage points less than their white counterpart. However, a black person with a PhD degree will actually be paid more than a white person with a comparable degree.

That is an interesting progression. However, just over 7 percent of all new PhDs in 2004 were African Americans,[3] but those statistics nevertheless demonstrate the value of education in practical terms. They also show the degree to which higher education and professional achievement are becoming the ticket to a better life for our people. We need to make sure every young person hears this: taking schoolwork seriously and making good grades isn't "acting white." It is simply showing that you care about making something of yourself. It is the most natural thing in the world, and it is an essential part of a happy and productive life.

It is tempting to think that the road to success in the black community is to continue the methods of the civil rights era. That seems to be the opinion of some of our most vocal black leaders who take the slightest hint of prejudice or bad judgment in the white community as an excuse for another march on Washington. But somebody needs to tell these misinformed voices that we are not in Selma anymore. The times have changed, and our methods need to change as well. But you won't hear this message from civil rights leaders, the liberal press, or even the NAACP.

One of the problems with the civil rights battles of the sixties that you don't hear much about is the fact that, early on, Leftists and anarchists crept into the civil rights movement, not because they cared about black folks and their problems in the least, but because they wanted to plant seeds of bitterness between the races in order to further their own political agenda, which was inspired and funded by the communists. The leaders of these groups were anti-Democratic and anticapitalist, and their goal was to bring America down.

This is the strand of militant activism that showed up in the Black Power movement and in self-styled revolutionaries such as Stokely Carmichael, H. Rap Brown, Amiri Baraka, and Malcolm X. These men weren't interested in peaceful coexistence; they were agitating for a violent overthrow of the government, which meant they were doomed from the start.

There is no doubt that a lot of good came from the work of the early civil rights leaders, particularly from Dr. King's brand of non-violence. Rosa Parks also is an example of this way of producing change. But the work done by the Left, turning blacks and whites against each other, often with greater violence than during the marches of the sixties, left a legacy of fear, anger, and distrust. At least part of the tension between the races today is due to the fact that people with bad ideas and dangerous motives abused the trust they were given, and they have done us all a great disservice.

LYNDON JOHNSON'S NIGHTMARE

Those who participated in the demonstrations and disturbances of the sixties welcomed the Left into the civil rights movement, I suspect, because of what they saw as the desertion of the Christian Right from the struggle. In the Deep South, Christians had an opportunity early on to embrace the civil rights movement, and they chose not to get involved. In fact, Dr. King's "Letter from the Birmingham Jail" was a response to the white ministers who said, in essence, "You're not from here, so don't bring your out-of-town problems to us."

For a long time, blacks were not welcomed in the traditional institutions of the South, including colleges, seminaries, and many kinds of public service. Most of the places that said, "Come on in here and we'll help you," were all liberal. In the absence of the influence of the moral base that is the natural home for most blacks, they opened the door for politically active blacks to be seduced by the Left. Blacks were looking for acceptance, and the presence of whites marching beside them in the face of police brutality was a public validation of what was happening in the culture at large. It was part of Dr. King's strategy to involve these people and, by so doing, to impact the conscience of the nation.

In his "I Have a Dream" speech, Dr. King said that the dream of blacks in America is "deeply rooted in the American Dream."[4] The words of the Declaration of Independence that "all men are created equal, and endowed by their Creator with certain unalienable rights" was a promise waiting to be fulfilled. He earned his bachelor's degree at Morehouse College, then went on to earn a PhD at a liberal white college, Boston University, so he had seen both worlds.

With that door propped open and the connections made between Dr. King and the liberal academics, an informal relationship between the political Left and the civil rights movement did come to pass. And because white conservatives had refused to join the cause, the leaders of the civil rights movement joined forces with liberal policy makers in government to try to speed up the process of change. But in many cases the collaboration proved to be ineffective and costly.

If you remember what happened with the issue of compulsory busing during the 1970s and 1980s, you may be able to see why so many whites took exception to the goals of the civil rights movement. Busing drove a wedge between blacks and whites by trying to force social programming down the throats of the majority white population before they had a chance to adapt naturally to all the changes that were taking place all around them.

The idea that government could force blacks and whites to coexist peacefully was another notion from Lyndon Johnson's Great Society era that relied more on sociology than real-world experience. The idea that fairness could be enforced by law began with *Brown v. Board of Education*. That ruling integrated the schools in Kansas and led to the end of "separate but equal" policies nationwide. However, that case inadvertently opened the door to other problems.

UNINTENDED CONSEQUENCES

Brown was a start, but there was resistance to government's attempts to impose its will on the public. If integration was not taking place fast enough to please the experts, the bureaucrats in the Johnson administration were determined to make it happen, even if they had to do it by force. The case of *Bradley v. Richmond School Board* (1974) was the first step in that direction, leading eventually to compulsory school busing nationwide.

In this case, the courts overturned local school board policies that simply acknowledged the status quo. Blacks and whites were living in separate communities, and their schools were naturally segregated. But to expedite the process of integration, the Supreme Court ordered the Richmond school district to begin busing black children into white neighborhoods.

This pattern continued throughout the seventies, as courts intervened in cities such as Boston, Cleveland, Los Angeles, and

Philadelphia. In Delaware and Indiana, black students were bused from inner-city districts to middle-class white districts in the suburbs. Predictably, resistance to these efforts, by whites as well as by many blacks, was intense. A county-wide busing program that had been instituted in Los Angeles public schools in 1978 had to be halted three years later when the citizens of California passed a referendum effectively ending busing in that state, except in cases where there was evidence of deliberate segregation.

Over the next ten years, several cases were filed in state courts over this issue, both pro and con, until the Supreme Court effectively ended further debate by refusing to hear a case in Virginia in which intentional resegregation was the issue. Then, the Court's ruling in a case from Oklahoma City in 1991 held that court-ordered busing could end if everything "practicable" had been done to eliminate school discrimination. Despite all the laws and judgments handed down over nearly two decades, it was obvious that busing wasn't working.

Forcing people to "do the right thing" by government mandate is a recipe for rebellion. While there was little in the way of actual physical confrontation over this issue, it soon became apparent that government's efforts to force the issue had accelerated the flight of white families away from places where busing was tried. This led, in turn, to the resegregation of many schools and added a new level of distrust and hostility between the races in some communities where it had not existed before the "experts" stepped in.

Major social changes take time. We should know by now that they cannot be forced. Over time there would be a natural assimilation as white and black students interacted more naturally and in their own way. In the schools my children attended, blacks and whites were completely intermingled. They hung out together, played sports together, and went to concerts together because they were allowed to get acquainted naturally over time. But many of the early civil rights initiatives were initiated in a heavy-handed manner and had unintended consequences.

Forced busing and forced assimilation were more than the white majority could deal with, so rather than bowing to government's demands, they picked up and left. Apparently it had never occurred to the experts that Americans are, by definition, freedom-loving people, and forced socialization is anything but free. As a result of twenty years of bad social policy, there are major cities in this country today where the school districts are 70, 80, or even 90 percent minority, because white families left town rather than bow to the intimidation.

TOWARD A NEW CONSENSUS

There is a new assimilation of whites and upwardly mobile, middle-class blacks taking place in most American cities today. But this time it is happening naturally as people become acquainted with each other through their schools, workplace, and churches. What the Great Society social engineers tried to accomplish through busing and other kinds of forced integration was, for the most part, a failure. Lyndon Johnson believed he could create the Great Society, and he used a Democrat-controlled Congress and the federal bureaucracy to force measures that could never have passed muster at the ballot box. There was no opportunity to evaluate what was working and what wasn't, so the American people simply said no.

One of the major problems with politics is that candidates get elected by making big promises. They don't get elected or funded if they say they want to keep the status quo or just make a few minor improvements. So they make big promises and offer all kinds of visionary programs, and when they get to Washington they create these legislative monstrosities that cost billions of taxpayer dollars and accomplish very little or make things worse.

That is part of what went wrong with the mandates of the civil rights era. Government's top-down solutions to problems in education, welfare, affirmative action, and poverty failed to deliver the goods. There has to be some response to the damage done by previous generations, but the response has to come naturally through human interaction, not by judicial fiat or by presidential executive orders.

On the other hand, there is a tendency for the white middle class to say, "We don't need to do anything. You people just need to lift yourself up by your own bootstraps." But, honestly, that is not enough. To say, "You've got a problem; deal with it!" doesn't work, and it certainly doesn't comport with Christian teaching.

If there is one thing we have learned from liberals, it is that government cannot mandate moral behavior. They have given it a shot, and it has not worked, and conservatives complain loudly that this is not the way to do it. There aren't many working models where conservatives have come forward with a better idea of how to make it work. It is as if they are saying, "You're on your own now, so fix it. And don't blame me if you fail!" There is something unsettling about this attitude for most African Americans, and we would like to think that the leaders of the evangelical movement may be beginning to finally understand.

On the other side, many blacks have not taken ownership of the generational transfer. One of the things we have learned from the controversy in Jena, Louisiana, in December 2006 is that the younger generation is still harboring the anger of the previous generation. Why didn't their mothers tell these kids, "Look, violence is not the answer! You've got to live together." But that takes us back to the issue of education and preparation for life in today's high-tech global society. Too many people in our neighborhoods don't have a grasp of their own history, the journey our people have made, or even the most basic history of this nation.

MOVING ON UP

Our young people need to be challenged to think about our history. What got our people out of slavery? Was it because our ancestors had the military might to overthrow the Confederate Army? Of course not. It was because white Christians moved upon by the Holy Spirit created the abolitionist movement. These men and women were intermediaries for the blacks. It is true that many blacks served in the military, and the movie *Glory* is a great example of what they did. But there would never have been an opportunity for a Glory Regiment to happen if there had not been a connection with benevolent whites who fought to end slavery.

When I was a young man, I would sometimes hear people say, "Young man, you're a credit to your race," or similar comments. Such statements weren't at all uncommon when I was growing up. But these kinds of remarks would be offensive to most blacks today. They feel that these comments imply that African Americans have to work harder to prove themselves, but whether we like it or not, it is true. We still do. Sometimes working a little harder can lead to some big rewards.

My private high school afforded me a great education, but I also learned some undesirable behaviors. When I got to school, I started hanging around with a group of kids who thought it was cool to talk this ghetto talk and use all kinds of slang. It wasn't long before my mother put a stop to that.

My mother, who was an elementary school teacher, never let me use slang at home. She believed that education was the way to a better life, and she wanted her children to speak as well as anyone. This was very much the same for immigrant families who came here from other countries and other traditions. Every ethnic group has tried to mainstream themselves linguistically, and my parents were no exception. They would say, "Harry, people are going to judge you by how you talk. So, at least in this house, we don't want you using that slang." And I understood that.

This, incidentally, is one of the issues that troubles me about the current wave of illegal immigration. There doesn't seem to be much effort on the part of many of these folks from Latin America to assimilate or to learn the common language. Regardless of what you believe about this issue, no one coming to this country can expect to be successful or share in the general prosperity of the nation unless they become fluent in English. That doesn't mean you have to lose your culture or your heritage. But if you want to get ahead, you have to learn the English language and the American culture.

I am reminded of another experience I had not long ago at an event with a lot of young people. There was an attractive black woman in her early thirties who told me her mother had said much the same thing that my mother said. This young woman was very articulate and clear in the way she spoke. She had braids in her hair, and she was wearing a funky outfit—she looked like a typical sister from the 'hood. But she had a wonderful gift for language, and at one point she said, "I speak two languages. I can speak Ebonics when I need to, or I can speak textbook English. That's the heritage I was given." I was glad to hear that. She understood that being proud of her heritage is good, but that doesn't mean she shouldn't also be able to succeed in the broader culture.

UNEQUAL OPPORTUNITY

Another issue that has been hotly debated over the past forty years is affirmative action. The term was first used in 1961, during the administration of John Kennedy, when the president authorized preferential hiring of minorities under Executive Order 10925. Subsequently, both public and private organizations were talking about establishing "quotas" and "set-asides," referring to the process of recruiting and hiring minority applicants. Kennedy's executive order was revolutionary in scope, but the original idea was quite simple.

The directive specified that federal contractors should take positive steps to insure that all Americans would have equal access to jobs and appointments "without regard to race, creed, color, or national origin." Though such issues had been addressed by both the Roosevelt and Truman administrations, this was the first time the government actually set out to change and monitor hiring practices based on race.

Today, nearly fifty years later, affirmative action has been used in everything from awarding government contracts to the hiring of corporate executives and public school teachers. Whites, Asian Americans, and others challenged the policy on the grounds that they were not being allowed to compete for jobs on the basis of merit. They claimed to be victims of "reverse discrimination." Affirmative action is still a hot-button issue, and this is another area that has led to antagonism between the races.

The origins of the affirmative action debate actually precede the Kennedy administration and, like the busing issue, can be traced back to the *Brown* decision, which was argued on the basis of the "equal protection" clause of the Fourteenth Amendment to the Constitution. In the Court's ruling on the case of Linda Brown, a black child who had been denied admission to an all-white school, Chief Justice Earl Warren presented the majority opinion, saying that "separate education facilities are inherently unequal." Segregating children solely on the basis of race, he said, "generates a feeling of inferiority as to their status in the community that may affect their hearts and minds in a way unlikely ever to be undone."[5]

Interpretations and extenuations of that ruling were later included in the Civil Rights Act of 1964 and Executive Order 11246, issued by President Johnson, which specifically mandated affirmative action hiring and promotion of minority faculty members at one of America's premier historically black colleges, Howard University. Because of delays in implementing these new policies, however, later administrations specified that goals and timetables should be established to insure compliance.

Over the years, there have been attempts to enforce quotas and proportional representation of minorities, but today the groups most affected by these rulings have questioned the ethical and legal consequences of continuing affirmative action forty years after the Civil Rights Act of 1964 and more than a hundred years after the Emancipation Proclamation.

When Martin Luther King Jr. challenged institutional racism in the fifties and sixties, he began by organizing voter registration drives throughout the South. He led rallies in his hometown of Albany, Georgia, in 1962, and then in Birmingham, Alabama, and Danville, Virginia, in 1963. He also organized the historic "March on Washington" in August 1963, where he spoke the words: "I have a dream that my four little children will one day live in a nation where they will not be judged by the color of their skin, but the content of their character."[6] His idea of change wasn't based on force but on the power of persuasion and the Christian's obligation to "honor one another."

A BETTER WAY

Those who felt that affirmative action created an unlevel playing field pointed out that the new laws weren't concerned about character but only the color of a person's skin. They argued that these practices were fundamentally unfair; however, Dr. King and others pointed out that the majority of blacks in this country were living in substandard housing, working at substandard jobs, and enduring substandard treatment at the hands of the white majority. If anything was unfair, that was. Affirmative action and financial assistance for the poor were merely an attempt to restore the balance. But none of those arguments would calm the storm of controversy that was rising in the land.

Part of the polarization of society at that time came down to the fact that many felt that affirmative action was being forced on an unwilling population by government edict rather than by reason or compassion on a human level. The main problem with the government's approach was the attempt to enforce not just equal opportunity but also equal results. Some people went so far as to imagine what would happen if that standard were applied in professional sports. But in the end, the attempt to enforce equal results proved hurtful to the men and women the affirmative action programs were meant to help by creating a hostile work environment and increasing the levels of distrust between whites and blacks.

Many of the problems of affirmative action in the workplace were repeated in schools and colleges where affirmative action admissions had been implemented. By placing minority students in academic settings for which they were unprepared, affirmative action enrollments guaranteed that many would fail. Until recently, only 40 percent of new freshmen at the University of California were admitted on the basis of academic merit. The other 60 percent were admitted primarily on the basis of race. However, in studies of student performance correlated by race at UC-Berkeley, just 27 percent of black students completed their degrees, compared to 66 percent of whites. At the elite universities most likely to give preferential admission to minority students, the dropout rate of nonwhites is consistently the highest.[7]

Such things should concern us, not just because of the problems created by the government's heavy-handed meddling, but also because the Christian tradition offers a better way. Those who believe in the founding principles of this nation, "that all men are created equal, that they are endowed by their Creator with certain unalienable rights," ought to understand the innate worth of all God's people of all races and national backgrounds. White society has been slow to accept this point of view, but policies that divide us on the basis of race, no matter how well meaning, don't do much for life, liberty, or happiness.

Rather than resorting to legal sanctions, we need to remember the words of the apostle Peter, who says in Acts, "God shows no partiality. But in every nation whoever fears Him and works righteousness is accepted by Him" (Acts 10:34–35). This challenge is repeated countless times in Scripture, that we are all equal in the eyes of God, and "partiality," or prejudice, is forbidden. As Paul says, "There is neither Jew nor Greek, there is neither slave nor free, there is neither male nor female; for you are all one in Christ Jesus" (Gal. 3:28).

Furthermore, we are told that nothing can separate us from the love of God. Paul goes on to say, "If you are Christ's, then you are Abraham's seed, and heirs according to the promise" (v. 29). In other words, we are commanded to live as equals, even when race, custom, and history would seem to divide us. If we are truly children of God, social programs based on behaviorist theories of enforced equality can be dangerous and counterproductive. That has often been the case. But if we will listen to the Word of God, there is a better way—that of love.

Sociologists can produce all kinds of economic and social data showing why affirmative action is a good idea. Furthermore, I do believe that some forms of affirmative action, by which black businesses are given an equal opportunity to compete for contracts or other ventures, are still needed. In the end it is not about equal opportunity; it is about our responsibility as Christians to live in accordance with what we say we believe. This is an area where the new black church can show the way. The Bible does not allow any place for ending prejudice by force. Rather, it tells us the law of God is written on the heart. (See Jeremiah 31:33.)[8]

THE TIPPING POINT

The commandment to love one another, as I said earlier, may be the hardest one for anyone to keep, and the history of our people would suggest it is impossible. But if it couldn't be done, Christ would never have commanded it. If we are willing to learn from our mistakes and look for new ways to work together, I believe miracles can happen. There is good sociological evidence for this in a recent best seller that confirms my premise. In his book *The Tipping Point*, Malcolm Gladwell writes about the process of change and describes how revolutionary changes take place in the natural order.

In the book, Gladwell shows how cultural trends change suddenly and dramatically when the right circumstances and players are in place. There are many factors that can set off a sudden change response: we see it medicine, in psychology, and especially in business, where a new fad can suddenly spread like wildfire. However, there are common factors in every case, in which these and other factors described by Malcolm Gladwell can be seen. When the environment is right, anything can change, suddenly and dramatically.[9]

For years, the underlying message from the Left has been that blacks and other minorities can't possibly make it on their own. Along with some of our black leaders who are still living in the twilight of the civil rights era, they have been saying that the majority culture is out to get us. They tell us we have to stay with "our people," trying to create an us-versus-them mentality. Most of all we are supposed to keep these self-appointed gatekeepers in power and the rest of the nation in turmoil so that we can get "our rights."

Conservatives, on the other hand, believe in the power of personal responsibility and self-determination. We believe that individuals, free from government interference and restrictions, can rise above their circumstances through hard work and self-discipline. The race hustlers tell us that conservatives are against the poor, but that is not true. As I have already shown in this book, conservatives turn out to be more generous in their giving than liberals, and Christian conservatives are the most generous of all. More importantly, conservatives believe that free enterprise, wealth creation, and upward mobility are every man's right and privilege, and those things cannot be mandated by government; they come through the dignity of work.

Clearly, the messages of the Left and the Right are in conflict, and a lot of people in the black community are stuck somewhere in between. We want to make our own way in the world and achieve great things, but we have been told that Uncle Sam is our only hope. We are told that Republicans don't care about poor people. Yet, instead of doing things to simplify our lives and remove the roadblocks that prevent our people from getting ahead, Democrats spend their time passing unconstructive bills like increasing the minimum wage, as if that is the answer to our problems. Sorry, but the minimum wage is for teenagers and low-wage workers with minimum skills. Is that the best they can do?

Giving a "tip" to people on the bottom rung of the economic ladder will not change conditions in the ghetto. Ghettos can only be changed by the moral renewal that happens within each individual human heart and by economic development that creates middle-class jobs in viable industries. Two years from now, all the effort spent on raising the minimum wage will not have any significance. Instead, like the old Wendy's commercial, we will be yelling, "Where's the beef?"

A few years ago, feminists were talking about breaking through the glass ceiling into corporate management. The media blew it up and tried to make corporate America the villain, saying they were holding back a generation of female executives. It turned out, however, that the only barrier holding women back was their own lack of preparation. When women who were motivated to enter the world of big business went and got the education and experience they needed to apply for those jobs, they got their shot. Today some of the most accomplished and highest paid executives in the country are women. And, believe me, those women earned those jobs by proving they could do the work, not by government mandates.

This is happening in the black community as well. Look, for example, at people like Herman Cain, the founder of Godfather's Pizza and an accomplished black business consultant, who achieved success based on his own fortitude and imagination. Such people aren't asking for handouts. They have broken through the racial glass ceiling and earned their success the old-fashioned way. Growing numbers of blacks hold positions as executives, mid-level managers, doctors, lawyers, and professionals in many fields. They are making a contribution to the community, and they are great examples of what motivated people can achieve. But to break free, we have to forget the labels and stereotypes that liberals have been putting on us for years.

THE POWER OF TRANSFORMATION

We need to understand that the tax-and-spend Democrats have not changed their stripes. The money they are spending comes out of your pocket too. If our people are content to live on handouts from government welfare, we will be defined by our poverty. But if we want to be defined by our skills and talents, then we need to start associating with people who believe in the benefits of free enterprise, personal responsibility, and prosperity.

Blacks and whites have to come together. For their part, whites need to take steps to cross the racial divide. They need to be willing to work with and for blacks in business, and they will need to elect more qualified blacks to public office. On the other hand, there will have to be some fundamental rethinking in the black community as well, especially about how long we intend to live under the thumb of politicians who, instead of making a place for us in the upper ranks of society, are busy making life more comfortable for us at the bottom.

The social programs of the sixties worked against us, and all the hot-button issues I have talked about in this chapter are part of the sixties' residue. Conservative Christians know that the federal government cannot change the evil nature of man. Only the gospel of Jesus Christ can change a human heart. Everything else is a temporary measure. Today, at the beginning of this new century, blacks and whites are beginning to discover the benefits of working together for the benefit of everyone.

The fact that between 10 and 20 percent of African Americans are willing to take a second look at their bondage to the Democratic Party, voting for morally responsible conservative candidates, is a great start.[10] The biggest sociological change of all may not be far behind. When we have a majority of principled, hard-working men and women in our communities, empowered by their faith in God and a commitment to personal responsibility, we will truly have reached a tipping point. Now that is something to look forward to.

The Way Forward

W HEN I OPENED MY EYES VERY EARLY ON THE MORNING
of February 3, 2006, my family informed me that the six-
and-a-half-hour surgery I had endured went smoothly. "They got
all the cancer!" my wife said with a smile. I had only been away
from them for a few hours, but it felt like months. Thirty staples
reconnected the tissue from my stomach up to my sternum. My
esophagus had been removed, my stomach stretched and reorga-
nized, and I was receiving all my food through a feeding tube.

It had been six months since I had been given a 15 to 20
percent chance of survival unless I went through this very sophisticated combination of chemotherapy, radiation, and surgery. This
surgery was like making it to an oasis in the desert. Now my survival prospects would quadruple. But for the first several months
there was always that nagging question in the back of my mind:
will I really make it? So when I woke up one morning in early
2007 and realized I had already made it through the first year, I
was filled with hope, believing I would be able to live a long and
healthy life.

But even as I reflect on my physical health, I have to pause to
ask myself, "What about the health of our country?" There is a lot
of good news, and changes are taking place that we ought to celebrate. Even so, there is also a great deal of dangerous pathology
out there. Relations between blacks and whites are better in some

places, but we are still not on the same page. The immigration crisis has thrown a whole new set of problems into the mix, and as the figures and statistics make all too clear, there are problems in the black community that often seem insurmountable. With godly counsel and a renewed commitment to our families and communities, I believe we can make it better. Still, I have to wonder, will we ever be able to heal the divisions in our land?

Black America needs the kind of renewal that comes from striving for exceptional personal achievement, strengthening our families, and building a legacy for future generations. It has become so clear to me that we have the capacity, here and now, to turn things around. The demagogues and race hustlers will tell us that we are down and out, that "the man" is robbing us of our inheritance and our only hope is to wage cultural warfare to get "our rights." Excuse me, but wasn't that last year's message? And the year before that too? Is that really the best they can come up with?

African Americans are about to become the second most prominent minority group in this country in the next few years. In five years or less, the Hispanic community will emerge as the most sought-after voting bloc. Because that community is not as predictable in its makeup or its voting patterns as blacks have been, it is only logical that Democrats and Republicans will wage an expensive tug-of-war for the Hispanic vote. At that point, the midnight callers won't be hanging around our door anymore. If we keep hanging out with Democrats who have been great at making promises and poor at bringing home the bacon, we will be stuck in the same old rut. Nothing will change until we make up our minds that we will not settle for the status quo anymore.

I have not always been a big fan of New Year's resolutions, but I made one this year. I made a commitment to become more effective, to offer a voice of reason regarding race relations and moral clarity in this nation. Because of all the physical and emotional struggles I have endured, I saw this as a personal challenge to bring healing to a philosophically divided nation. So today I am motivated by two things: the needs of black America—social, political, and moral—and a deep personal desire to make a lasting impact on my world.

A New Resolution

The Katrina tragedy ought to be a dramatic warning to blacks that communities that have allowed themselves to languish in poverty for many years can be utterly destroyed by natural disasters or by a sudden economic crisis. We can no longer labor under the assumption that all we have to do is cry, "Racist!" and the cavalry will ride to our rescue. The cavalry of government help and social-welfare programs will never take us where we need to go. Handouts will never give us what we really need. From now on, we are going to have to be our own cavalry!

If you have traveled with me through these pages and been moved by anything I have said, then I would encourage you to join me in a new resolution. Let's make a resolution that we will not fall into the emotional trap of blaming "the man" for all our problems. There have always been racism and prejudice in the world—yes, it's wrong and it needs to stop, but we cannot afford to let it stop us. Personal and institutional racism will be overcome by black achievement. We can serve in positions of authority where we can help determine the future direction of the nation if we are willing to pay the price. But we will do it the old-fashioned way, as the Smith-Barney commercials used to say: we'll *earn* it.

With God's help, we will save ourselves by achieving personal success that affects our community. If I am a businessman, I will need to understand that I have both an economic mission and a cultural mission, creating jobs, wealth, and influence not just for myself but for my community. If I am a working mother or a full-time homemaker, I will need to understand that my family is forever. As someone said, my kids are the only thing I can take to heaven with me when I die. They are my legacy to the world, and the most important responsibility I will ever have. *Please, God, let me raise them and love them and teach them that they are*

beautiful in Your eyes, and they must not be sucked down into the
sewers of today's trash-filled ghetto culture.

When my father sat me down to give me my inheritance of a
good education, I knew that all he wanted in return for his legacy
was that I would become the best I could be at whatever profes-
sion I chose. I specifically remember him saying that I could be a
janitor, a construction worker, a doctor, or a lawyer, but he wanted
me to promise to be the best I could be, whichever path I chose.

I am sure I let my father down on quite a few occasions. On the
other hand, his visionary investment during a time of great national
stress—due to racial unrest, the Vietnam War, and so many other
socially traumatic upheavals during those years—helped prepare me
to attend some of the finest schools in the country. Dad's gift helped
prepare me for my undergraduate work at Williams College and
later my MBA at Harvard. That was a gift I can never fully repay.

JUSTICE ISSUES

More than the education, however, what my father gave me was
the knowledge that my future was in my own hands. He and my
mother could feed and clothe me, and they could take care of my
needs, but they could not give me success. That would be up to
me. As I think about the crisis of values in this country, and all
the social and moral tensions we face each day, I feel that I must
share this important lesson with as many people as I can. We are
in charge of our own success, and what we do today will determine
how we live tomorrow.

America is at a crossroads. Whether or not our democracy can
last another two hundred years will be decided in the first twenty
years of this century. I believe the new black church is uniquely
poised to help the entire nation develop innovative ways of dealing
with complex racial and cultural issues. There is no doubt that
adjustments will have to be made to heal the divisions. The gap
between blacks and whites is a greater concern than the ethnic
controversies on our Southern borders. The one catalyst that can

unite the races in America is the Christian church.

Fifty years ago, the national evangelical movement missed a great opportunity to help direct the civil rights movement. If the white church in the South had preached against racism and called for local churches to lead the movement for justice on biblical grounds, they could have helped navigate the nation through many strife-filled years. The church of the 1950s opted, instead, to maintain the status quo. They could have led the nation through a very delicate transition, but now that task falls to us.

What happened in the little town of Jena, Louisiana, in December 2006 captured the attention of the nation for a while. In the beginning, new reports from the scene were saying that white kids at the local high school were angry that black students had the nerve to sit in the shade of what was known as "the white tree," where white students would congregate during lunch hour and after school. To show their displeasure, white students began hanging nooses in places where the black kids and their families would go.

The news reports went on to say that the situation in Jena escalated rapidly until one day a black student named Mychal Bell jumped one of the white students named Justin Purvis, and, with five of his buddies, beat him badly. There followed talk of shotguns and race riots, and in the blink of an eye fifteen thousand demonstrators descended on that tiny town, urged on by none other than Jesse Jackson and Al Sharpton. Jackson flew down to meet with the now famous "Jena Six" and their supporters, demanding an inquiry into the way the case was being handled by the police and threatening to sue the county prosecutor for bringing charges against Mychal Bell for beating up Justin Purvis.

At that point, things went crazy. The Jena Six became overnight celebrities, making stops on all the New York and Washington talk shows and cable networks. When I first wrote about it for my column at Townhall.com, I said, "The story is so mired in twists and turns that, at first blush, it sounds more like a sophisticated screenplay than a real life story."[1] As it turns out, mine was a pretty good assessment. The more we learn about what actually happened in Jena, the more we discover that this particular narrative is not exactly what actually happened.

It is true that there were verbal and physical confrontations, and I have no doubt that a generational animus does exist in Jena, as it does in many other small Southern towns. It is also true that there were fist fights and nooses and shotguns, but it was not, as the media and the outside agitators would have us believe, a race war that had been brewing for generations. Craig Franklin, who is the assistant editor of the local newspaper, *The Jena Times*, covered the story from day one, then published a detailed summary of the events that actually took place in a lengthy story in the *Christian Science Monitor*.[2]

Franklin's retelling does not remove all doubt, and it does not have a happy ending. It reminds us that we ought to be careful before leaping into the flames of controversy. There are always two sides to every story, and, I am sorry to say, there are always agitators who are only too quick to jump into these explosive situations to excite racial tensions for their own benefit. This makes it all the harder to deal with the serious social problems that trouble the black community today, including especially the single most troubling, crime and punishment.

CRIME AND PUNISHMENT

There are now more than two million prisoners in the criminal justice system in this country, with four million others either on probation, parole, or awaiting trial, and the majority in every category are black. Dr. Manning Marable is a professor of political science and African American studies at Columbia University in New York. I am sure his views and mine on most of the issues in this book would be quite different, as he is a liberal Democrat. Recently I had a chance to read a speech he delivered at Fayetteville State University, in North Carolina, concerning the unequal enforcement of justice in this country and its effects on the black community. I would like to recap some of what he said.

In 1974, the number of people in state prisons in this country stood at 187,500. By 1991, that number had risen to 711,700. Just under two-thirds of those men and women had less than a high-school education, and one-third of them were unemployed at the time of arrest. By the end of the 1980s, incarceration rates were soaring, especially for blacks. By December 1989, the total number of inmates in federal and state prisons totaled just over a million— that is roughly one out of every 250 Americans in jail.

For African Americans, however, the rate was over 700 per 100,000, or about seven times that of whites. Half of all prisoners were black; 23 percent of all black males in their twenties were either in prison, on parole, on probation, or awaiting trial. In the last year of that decade, there were more African Americans in jail than the total number of blacks living under apartheid in South Africa.[3]

In New York, African Americans and Latinos made up approximately 25 percent of the total population in the 1990s; but by 1999, as Dr. Marable reports, 83 percent of all prisoners and 94 percent of all individuals convicted on drug offenses in that state were from these two groups. There is no doubt that many of those arrested and convicted were guilty as charged. There is also a pattern of racial bias, confirmed by the U.S. Commission on Civil Rights, which found that while African Americans make up about 14 percent of all drug users nationally, they accounted for 35 percent of all drug arrests, 55 percent of all drug convictions, and 75 percent of all prison admissions for drug offenses.

Currently, the racial proportions of those under some type of correctional supervision, including parole and probation, are one in fifteen for young white males, one in ten for young Latino males, and one in three for African American males. If you extrapolate those numbers out, it is statistically feasible that as many as eight out of every ten African American males can expect to be arrested at some point in their lifetime.

These are, as I have said repeatedly, troubling statistics, and they raise many troubling questions. How do we begin to address all the problems these numbers imply? Dr. Manning's answer is one I happen to share. He told his audience in North Carolina that the answer is a restoration and rehabilitation program developed by Christians and secular sociologists called "restorative justice." As some readers will know, this is also a program that has been pioneered in the prison system by Prison Fellowship Ministries and its founder, Chuck Colson. It is also being taught today in more traditional academic settings.

A New Kind Justice

The goal of restorative justice, in Dr. Marable's words, is to bring back from the margins millions of Americans who are denied jobs due to prior felony convictions, to bring back millions of African Americans who are excluded from exercising their right to vote, and to bring ex-prisoners back into the community and the local economy by eliminating state-sanctioned restrictions on the kinds of jobs that former prisoners can hold.

Restorative justice programs often include a program of "therapeutic jurisprudence," which focuses more on rehabilitation than mere punishment. According to the liberal advocacy group Human Rights Watch, there are approximately 1,976,019 men and women incarcerated in adult prisons today. Of those, 1,239,946, or 63 percent, are either black or Latino. These two groups make up about 25 percent of the total U.S. population; yet they're doing 63 percent of the hard time. What this tells me is that, first, we have a problem with crime in our neighborhoods, but, second, it tells me we have a problem with unequal enforcement of the laws.[4]

When these men and women come home, wouldn't it be a good idea for them to be ready to go back to work, to rejoin their families and communities, and to get their lives back on track? Too often, they have only been trained to be better criminals, and because of the treatment they have received from the criminal justice system, they have become hardened and bitter and more violent than ever. Restorative justice works at both ends of the cycle, helping to make sure that the laws and sentencing requirements fit the crime and helping ex-prisoners return to a productive life.

Restorative justice works inside the penal system to help prisoners make restitution to their victims, to understand that their crime is bigger and more serious than they may have known because of the human dimensions of the crime. It helps them to make the adjustment back into society when they have done their time. The following list, from Dr. Ron Claassen of the Peace and Conflict Center at Fresno Pacific College, describes the ten original principles of the restorative justice process.[5]

Restorative Justice

1. Crime is primarily an offense against human relationships and secondarily a violation of a law (since laws are written to protect safety and fairness in human relationships). When we place the emphasis on the violation of law instead of the violation of the human relationship, we hide or mask the real violation. It is possible for an offender to be tried and sentenced for an offense, more or less serious, and never be fully aware of the human consequences or impact of the violation.

2. Restorative justice recognizes that crime (violation of persons and relationships) is wrong and should not occur and also recognizes that after it does, there are dangers and opportunities. The danger is that the community, victim(s), and/or offender emerge from the response further alienated, more damaged, disrespected, disempowered, feeling less safe and less cooperative with society. The opportunity is that the injustice is recognized, the equity is restored (restitution and grace), and the future is clarified so participants are safer, more respectful, and more empowered and cooperative with each other and society.

3. Restorative justice is a process to make things as right as possible and includes: attending needs created by the offense such as safety and repair of injuries, relationships, and

physical damage resulting from the offense; and attending needs related to the cause of the offense (addictions, lack of social or employment skills or resources, lack of understanding or will to make moral or ethical decisions, etc.).

4. The primary victim(s) of a crime is the one(s) most impacted by the offense. The secondary victims are others impacted by the crime and might include family members, friends, criminal justice officials, community, etc.

5. As soon as immediate victim, society, and offender safety concerns are satisfied, restorative justice views the situation as a teachable moment for the offender—an opportunity to encourage the offender, to learn new ways of acting and being in community. If there is not some constructive intervention to encourage the voluntary change with the first-, second-, and third-time offender, the likelihood is higher that they will become part of the group that is unable or unwilling to control their impulses to hurt people. Therefore, it seems both efficient and humane (and biblical: see both Galatians 6:1 and Matthew 5) to design a restorative justice system that provides interventions that address the needs of both victim and offender and encourage voluntary and cooperative change.

6. Restorative justice prefers responding to the crime at the earliest point possible and with the maximum amount of voluntary cooperation and minimum coercion since healing in relationships and new learning are voluntary and cooperative processes.

7. Restorative justice prefers that most crimes are handled using a cooperative structure including those most impacted by the offense as a community to provide support and accountability. This might include primary and secondary victims and family (or substitutes if they choose not to participate), the offender and family, community representatives, government representatives, faith community representatives, school representatives, etc.

8. Restorative justice recognizes that not all offenders will choose to be cooperative. Therefore there is a need for outside authority to make decisions for the offender who is not cooperative. The actions of the restorative justice authorities and the consequences imposed should be tested by whether they are reasonable, restorative, and respectful (for victim[s], offender, and the community).

9. Restorative justice prefers that offenders who are not yet cooperative be placed in settings where the emphasis is on safety, values, ethics, responsibility, accountability, and civility. They should be exposed to the impact of crime on victims, invited to learn empathy for the victim, and offered learning opportunities to become equipped with skills to be a productive member of society. They should be continually invited (not coerced) to become cooperative with society and given the opportunity to demonstrate this in appropriate settings as soon as possible.

10. Restorative justice requires follow-up and accountability structures utilizing the natural community as much as possible since keeping agreements is the key to building a trusting community.

TRUTH AND RECONCILIATION

Restorative justice is one of the best ways I know to work on both sides of the crime and punishment dilemma, and I would love to see programs like this in every jail and prison in America. A related issue is the need for reconciliation, bringing offenders and their victims together to heal old wounds and begin the process of renewal. One of the most powerful examples of this is going on now in South Africa, where the horrors of state-approved apartheid led to intense bitterness and hatred between the races.

Pastor Jerome Liberty is a protégé of mine and director of Victory Ministries International in Port Elisabeth, South Africa. Growing up in that racially divided country, he witnessed many heartbreaking atrocities. On one of my trips to visit with him and his associates, Jerome told me about the Truth and Reconciliation Commission. It had been set up to help produce healing and renewal to the country by bringing those who had suffered under apartheid together with their oppressors. The commission understood that to move forward they first had to deal with the past and then come to an agreement on how they could cooperate under the new system.

There was an equal and open exchange where both sides could talk back and forth about what they went through, and people who had been leaders in the former government were allowed to say what they did without fear of punishment. Some individuals admitted to abuse and torture and other kinds of victimization, and as much as you would think that would be alienating, what happened was they wept and they forgave.

During the 1990s, the Truth and Reconciliation Commission chaired by Archbishop Desmond Tutu granted amnesties to some of the perpetrators of violence and human rights abuses. Some had to face prosecution for their crimes, but the objective was to clear the slate and get rid of the anger and hatred that had existed for centuries. One of the most amazing things I heard was the story of a man named Adriaan Vlok, who was the Minister of Law and Order under the old government in the late 1980s. He was the highest-ranking member to apply for amnesty for crimes committed by the state.

After confessing to ordering the 1988 bombing of the offices of the South African Council of Churches, he received amnesty for that offense but would have to face charges on other counts. However, one morning Mr. Vlok, who is white, walked into the Union Buildings in Pretoria, went to the office of the director-general and said he wanted to offer a personal apology to the Reverend Frank Chikane, who is black.

When he entered Rev. Chikane's office, according to a BBC report, he produced a Bible with the words, "I have sinned against the Lord and against you, please forgive me" (John 13:15), inscribed on the cover. He handed it to Rev. Chikane and pleaded for forgiveness for his sin against him. At that point, Vlok opened his bag, took out a bowl and two towels, and insisted on washing Rev. Chikane's feet. Rev. Chikane had been head of the South African Council of Churches in 1989 and was a leading antiapartheid activist. He had also been the target of other assassination attempts. But this time Adriaan Vlok had come in peace. Subsequently, Vlok was invited to preach in Rev. Chikane's church in Soweto.[6]

The Truth and Reconciliation Commission was empowered to investigate and clear up incidents that had happened over the long history of apartheid and, whenever possible, to work together for healing and restoration. Part of the release was the truth telling. It wasn't a secret what had happened, but the truth telling allowed them to deal with it openly and reach a point of healing. Perhaps that is what needs to happen in Jena, Louisiana. If they would put together that kind of commission on a less formal basis, I am sure it could be very powerful.

Truth telling is key to forgiveness. The Christian model of forgiveness calls for recognition, repentance, and then restitution of some sort. Then there has to be a restoration of relationships and a renewal, at which point you move into the area of being totally reconciled. I would say that reconciliation is critical, and the organization that is in the best position to do that is the church.

JUSTICE AND JUDGMENTALISM

There is a lot more that could be said about justice and judgmentalism, but I offer an example from my own experience. At one point in my ministry I had to come to grips with my own sins of racism and judgmentalism. Several years ago when I was a younger man, I received a pastoral call to a small town in western New York. It was a call to start a new church in a white community, and my wife and I felt led to accept the mission.

The black population was less than 2 percent in the whole region, and that concerned me a little, but I agreed to start the church. There were only 20 to 25 people when we first got started, and most of those who attended were honest working folks. They were not the typical middle-class whites, but blue collar and other working families, many of whom were struggling to make ends meet. They had many of the same problems of poor black folks, but some of the attitudes were troubling to me and I am afraid I did not respond very well.

My biggest surprise was realizing that I had race issues. Mine were more class oriented. At least since the seventh grade, the white people I had dealt with were generally educated people. Many were intellectuals and high achievers, and I got along fine in that environment. Suddenly, here I was with folks who were struggling, who walked and talked and dressed like working people, and I realized I had a problem with poor white folks.

Here I was, a black minister and a man of the cloth, and I had some attitudes that were totally inappropriate. I realized it was something I was going to have to deal with. It was during a powerful Communion service one evening in Atlanta, and the Lord started speaking to me about racial prejudice. I was deeply touched in my spirit, so I prayed and repented. I had accepted the call to go wherever the Lord sent me, and He sent us to preach to a lot of impoverished white folks, people who were in need of financial help, and this root of bitterness came to the surface.

I remember thinking, "You've got to be kidding me! You guys have had all the breaks! You've had all the advantages this society can provide, and yet you're struggling and can't make it on your own! What's your excuse?" I admit, I am ashamed of it now, but I could not help it. I was saying to myself, "My people have had this problem forever. If we'd had just half the opportunities available to you, man, what they could have done!"

Once I faced up to what I had been doing, I became a different person. God did a work in my heart and, most remarkable of all, as the changes happened in me, the church began to grow. The church was 98 percent white. Some of those people were disowned by their families because they attended a church pastored by a black man. Many of them were paying a tithe. Some of them were Italian with a Roman Catholic background; others were just garden variety heathens when they came to us. But at the end of the day I learned that reconciliation can happen if people's hearts are truly changed.

LIFE LESSONS

It was in that little town of Coming, New York, that I discovered that the church can come together and be a powerful voice in the community. I pastored there for about seven years, and the Lord raised the church to became a major unifying voice in the broader body of Christ in that area. That church still helps to organize regional and city-wide events bringing God's people together in a spirit of brotherhood and reconciliation. They are some of the nicest people in the world.

Toward the end of my ministry there, I was invited on a missions trip to Germany. During that event, I was praying, "Lord, I'll go anywhere You send me." I had a very successful trip to Germany, and I was ministering in the middle of the antiblack region of the country. In fact, our meetings were held in a former SS headquarters built for Adolf Hitler. My uncle who had served in Germany during the Second World War had often talked to me about what Hitler had done and how the Nazis hated blacks. So I had all these negative images in my mind about the country, but when I returned I felt as if the Lord was asking me, "Harry, are you willing to go wherever I send you?"

When I got back home to New York, I suddenly felt out of place. I remember thinking, "What am I doing here?" I believe the Lord was telling me that I had accomplished my mission in that city and it was time for another challenge, and that precipitated my leaving the church. Within a few weeks I received a call to go to the church where I currently minister near Washington DC, and that has opened a whole new chapter in my life.

Now I was to take over a church that was multiracial—70 percent black and about 30 percent white. At that time, nobody was talking much about the issue of racial reconciliation or how you deal with that. I don't think most people thought it was a very big issue. There are black churches and white churches, and that is just the way it is. But when my family and I moved to Maryland, we had the exact opposite situation from what we had had in New York. The blacks were in the majority and the whites were a minority.

In New York I hadn't talked much about race, but I talked a lot about the importance of unity. I suspect my presence in the pulpit each week said enough about race. But in Washington I felt that we had to address these issues because the racial tension was much greater there. As I studied these racial problems and talked to the leaders in our church about the environment in that city, I began to see racial conflict in a whole new light.

The dilemma of the black middle class is that it identifies with the white middle class and wants to participate more fully in the American Dream—which means wealth building. But the focus of the black political system tends to be toward the lowest rungs of society. When I look at the polls, comparing the way blacks and whites view the various presidential candidates, it is interesting to see how many blacks like what they are hearing from Senator Barack Obama. He is speaking to issues that blacks are concerned about. He is trying to be open to the poor, but he says there can also be financial advances for middle-class blacks as well.

The fact that his candidacy has been taken seriously tells us that upwardly mobile blacks have a place at the table. When you think about Jesse Jackson revving up the crowds down in Jena, you see someone who is down there dealing with the worst possible situation, which is poverty, anger, and violence, and that is the focus of his political clout. There is nothing that builds and promotes advancement. He is all attack and vilification with no grounds for reconciliation. That is yesterday's battle. Today we need a new philosophical framework.

DEALING WITH DIFFERENCES

It is interesting that Jerry Falwell died on the same day that Yolanda King died. Jerry Falwell had been the foremost spokesman for the Moral Majority and conservative views of the religious Right. As the daughter of Martin Luther King Jr., Yolanda King was an important voice for the ongoing struggle for civil rights. But in a sense, both of these movements are dead today. They need to be revitalized with a passing of the baton, but when they come back they will need to be different—and better.

I happened to be in Washington on the day they died. I was standing at the counter of a popular soul food restaurant down-town, waiting for a to-go order, when the news came across the television that Jerry Falwell had died. One of the waitresses looked over at the TV and said, "Wow, Jerry Falwell died." Then a black woman standing behind me spoke up loudly and with a certain ring to her voice, "Yeah, and I'm not mad about it!" Then she added, "He's going to be surprised when he wakes up!"

A lot of people laughed, but what she was saying was that Jerry Falwell claimed to be a man of God but he didn't really care about her or her problems. It wasn't that he had done anything in partic-ular, but it was a generalized criticism of those who say one thing and practice something else. In this case, it was a woman from the black community expressing her resentment about justice issues and the inner-city concerns she felt that Jerry Falwell and the Moral Majority never addressed.

It was as if she were saying, "If you're all that much of a Christian, then how come you let little kids go hungry? Or how can there not be equal opportunities for employment and jobs?" She was in a low-end job in a restaurant and probably lived in poor circumstances in an inner-city neighborhood, so all of her disappointment and resentment was dumped at the door of Jerry Falwell. That wasn't fair, but that is what she meant.

In the same way, when someone tells you that he is right and you are wrong, but it turns out he has been engaging in things that are morally reprehensible, you not only discover that this person is a hypocrite and not to be trusted, but you also become suspicious of everyone who shares his point of view. This was what was happening when the scandal involving Senator Larry Craig of Idaho became such a media circus. The behavior he was alleged to be practicing in secret was in such dramatic contrast to the policies he was defending on the Senate floor. Whatever happens in that case reflects poorly on his party and raises suspicions of hypocrisy.

The Bible says that judgment must begin at the house of God (1 Pet. 4:17). Those who claim to be God-fearing men and women are not above judgment. They ought to be especially cautious with their words and actions, because sooner or later the truth will be revealed and what people believe about them and their cause will be affected. Jesus warned His disciples about the evils of hypocrisy, saying, "For there is nothing covered that will not be revealed, nor hidden that will not be known. Therefore whatever you have spoken in the dark will be heard in the light, and what you have spoken in the ear in inner rooms will be proclaimed on the housetops" (Luke 12:2–3).

We saw the same sort of reaction on the day the verdict was announced in the O. J. Simpson case in California. After months of sensational testimony and theatrics by both sides, the jury was finally sequestered. When they came back, they declared that O. J. was not guilty of the murders of his ex-wife and her friend Ron Goldman. But what shocked the nation more than the verdict was the dramatic difference in the reactions of blacks and whites.

Whites, by and large, were outraged by the verdict. For them, everything from O. J.'s initial attempt to escape to Mexico to the DNA evidence at the crime scene cried out for a guilty verdict. But the reaction of the black community was exactly the opposite, and there were scenes from the courtroom, from the streets, and from many other places where people were glued to the television. Black people were cheering and yelling and jumping up and down. It was one of the most dramatic moments in modern history, and it demonstrated just how massive the divide was between blacks and whites.

Whites were convinced that O. J. had violated their trust. He had been a popular athlete with an impressive career in the National Football League, and he was loved and admired by everyone. But apparently he had a vicious temper, and it appeared that he had killed his white wife and a friend in the most brutal way imaginable. Now he was getting away with it. For many blacks, however, the O. J. verdict was a victory over what they perceived to be the overall injustice of the legal system in this country. Even if he was guilty, being pronounced not guilty was payback for all the injustice black people have suffered at the hands of the law.

RENEWED EXPECTATIONS

Let me be quick to say that no one condones what O. J. Simpson may have done. Thanks in part to revelations in the book written by O. J. and published by the Goldman family, called *If I Did It*, there is more reason now to believe that he did it than ever. But the response of blacks on that day was predictable. I know from my own experience that there is still a lot of deeply ingrained racism on both sides, and that was the main factor in the way people reacted.

When I was growing up, I remember hearing my mother and father say that a black person has to be twice as good to go half as far in their professional life as the typical middle-class white. That mind-set was not depressing to them, however. I think it was actually a motivator. They said, "I'm going to be the best I can be!" They raised us with the confidence that their kids would live in a better America—an America that would be enriched by their contributions. They knew intuitively that government's answers never trickle down to the personal level quickly enough to change anybody's life, and they weren't waiting for that.

My goal throughout this book has not been to attack any person or group or to raise alarms, but to offer a voice of hope and an exhortation to my fellow countrymen to find a better way.

There is a lot we can do through the political process to make improvements in our communities and our nation, but it is time now for the black community to raise the bar on personal achievement. It is time for a new beginning.

We need to set our sights a little higher, and we need to start thinking about the kind of investment we are prepared to make in the next generation. Today's black community is just comfortable enough that it is at risk of losing the drive and determination to change the cultural and social landscape. I might even say that some of us are suffering from cultural obesity: we are living too high, and it is high time we get ourselves back to the fitness center.

I remember the words spoken by James Brown several years ago, "I am black, and I am proud." But just remembering those words today makes me wonder: *What is the coming generation of young blacks doing now that will allow them to say those words and mean it?* What are they doing that would even justify those words—not just their ego, not just their arrogance or cockiness, but the kind of achievement they can really be proud of?

When I made that New Year's resolution I mentioned at the beginning of this chapter, I had a pretty good idea what I wanted to accomplish. I knew that my faith and values were inseparable and that a message of hope for all God's people would have to be the cornerstone of my ministry. I am still striving for that goal, but my prayer today is that men, women, and children in the black community all over this great nation will begin to work together as never before to find new and better solutions to our problems.

As I said earlier, the bigotry of low expectations has spread far beyond the ghetto, and there are many people who would be satisfied if things just remained the same. We are used to the way things are, and we can deal with the disruptions that come along from time to time. We will just do our business then head on back to the neighborhood where everybody looks alike and thinks alike and votes alike, and the same heartbreaking problems will just go on forever. Is that what we really want? I don't think so.

Martin Luther King Jr. was a prophet, and prophets never have an easy time of it. For as long as God has spoken through His servants, the prophets, they have been hunted and hated and killed for speaking the truth. Yet the lessons they teach us live on and have a way of changing everything, one way or the other. In the beginning of this book I included a quote from Dr. King that expressed his greatest wish, that one day all who work for a living will be one, with no thought to their separateness. For him, that wish would remain a dream unfulfilled. For us, it is a vision of what must be.

In that spirit, I commend this volume to you, wherever you may be in the journey, in the hope that you may join me in working for the day when the people of this great nation will truly be one, with no thought of our separateness—and looking always to the author and finisher of our faith, whose truth is eternal and unchanging.

■ ■ ■ ■

NOTES

[INTRODUCTION] A PROPHETIC MOMENT

1. Martin Luther King Jr., *Strength to Love* (New York: Harper & Row, 1963), 31.

2. Charlotte Allen, "Jena: The Case of the Amazing Disappearing Hate Crime," *The Weekly Standard*, January 21, 2008, http://www.weeklystandard .com/Content/Public/Articles/000/000/014/589bfhgz.asp (accessed January 18, 2008).

3. George Will, "Get Over It: Meaningless Racial Politics," Washington Post Writers Group, January 17, 2008.

4. Roddie A. Burris, "Jackson Slams Obama for 'Acting White,'" *The State* (South Carolina), September 19, 2007. Frederic U. Dicker, "'Jealous' Rev. Al Blasts Barack," *New York Post*, March 12, 2007. See Harry R. Jackson, "Sharpton and Jackson: Biggest Losers in Iowa, New Hampshire, and...," Townhall.com, January 7, 2008, http://www .townhall.com/columnists/HarryRJacksonJr/2008/01/07/sharpton_and_jackson_ biggest_losers_in_iowa,_new_hampshire,_and (accessed March 4, 2008).

5. Tony Vega, "Barack Obama's Church Honors Nation of Islam Leader Louis Farrakhan," Associated Content, January 8, 2008, http://www.associatedcontent .com/article/528635/barack_obamas_church_honors_nation.html (accessed February 18, 2008).

6. Nicholas Wapshott, "Obama Fails to Quell Row Over an Anti-Gay Singer," *New York Sun*, October 26, 2007, http://www.nysun.com/article/65297?page_no=1 (accessed February 18, 2008).

7. Martin Luther King Jr., *Stride Toward Freedom: The Montgomery Story* (New York: Harper, 1958), 36.

[CHAPTER ONE] THE NEW BLACK CHURCH

1. Harry R. Jackson Jr., *The Black Contract With America on Moral Values: Protecting America's Moral Compass* (Lake Mary, FL: Charisma House, 2005).

2. Senator Sam Brownback with Jim Nelson Black, *From Power to Purpose: A Remarkable Journey of Faith and Compassion* (Nashville, TN: Thomas Nelson, 2007), 94.

3. Harry R. Jackson Jr., "New Black Church on Election Day," *New York Sun*, November 2, 2004, http://nysun.com/article/4149 (accessed March 4, 2008).

4. Tom Hamburger and Peter Wallsten, "GOP Sees a Future in Black Churches: Social Issues Are Binding the Party With a Group Once Firmly in the Democratic Camp," *Los Angeles Times*, February 1, 2005, A1. *NB:* The first paragraph of the article said it all: "By courting conservative blacks in battleground states—reaching out through programs such as the president's faith-based initiative—GOP organizers believe they made the difference that secured [Bush]'s victory in 2004. In Ohio, for instance, a concerted effort increased black support for Bush from 9% in 2000 to 16% in 2004, providing a cushion that allowed the president to win the pivotal state outright on election night. *The Black Contract With America* will be unveiled by Bishop Harry R. Jackson Jr., a registered Democrat from suburban Washington who backed Bush in 2004 after voting against him four years earlier. He was drawn, he said, to the GOP's social conservatism that he thought reflected the true values of black churches."

5. Newt Gringrich et al., *Contract With America: The Bold Plan by Rep. Newt Gringrich, Rep. Dick Armey, and the House Republicans to Change the Nation*, Ed Gillespie and Bob Schellhas, ed. (New York: Times Books, 1994).

6. Market Strategies, "Ohio Statewide Survey: Equal Right, No Special Rights," March 25–28, 2004. Market Strategies; 20255 Victor Pkwy., Ste. 400; Livonia, Michigan 48152.

7. Kurt Jacobsen, "Tin Foil Hats, the MSM, and Election Mischief," http://www .logosjournal.com/issue_4.1/jacobsen.html (accessed March 6, 2008).

8. Market Strategies, "Ohio Statewide Survey."

9. Ibid.

[CHAPTER TWO] TEARING DOWN WALLS

1. Jackson, "New Black Church on Election Day."

2. Jerry Price, for the Ethics & Religious Liberty Commission, Southern Baptist Convention. "Racial Reconciliation," February 6, 2006, http://erlc.com/article/racial -reconciliation-african-american (accessed November 14, 2007). This report states, in part, that: "African Americans are more likely than average to say that they are ' born-again Christians.' A belief held by 57 percent of African Americans compared to 39 percent of adults nationwide (2001)."

3. Peter Kirsanow, "The 92% Solution: Kerry and the Black Vote," National Review Online, October 28, 2004, http://www.nationalreview.com/comment/ kirsanow200410280838.asp (accessed February 18, 2008).

4. ThinkExist.com, "Lord Palmerston Quotes," http://en.thinkexist.com/quotes/ Lord_Palmerston/ (accessed February 18, 2008).

5. George Barna and Harry R. Jackson Jr., *High-Impact African-American Churches: Leadership Concepts From Some of Today's Most Effective Churches*, (Ventura, CA: Regal Books, 2004).

6. Ibid.

7. The White House, "Fact Sheet: President Bush Announces Five-Year, $30 Billion HIV/AIDS Plan," June 8, 2007, http://www.whitehouse.gov/infocus/hivaids/ (accessed September 15, 2007).

[CHAPTER THREE] CIVIL RIGHTS AND WRONGS

1. Department of Health and Human Services, Administration for Children and Families, "Marriage, Divorce, Childbirth, and Living Arrangements Among African American or Black Populations," May 25, 2006, http://www.acf.hhs.gov/ healthymarriage/about/aami_marriage_statistics.htm (accessed November 21, 2007). See also: Maryann Reid, "First Comes Baby, Then Comes Marriage," *Christian Science Monitor*, April 24, 2006, http://www.csmonitor.com/2006/0424/p09s02-coop.html (accessed November 11, 2007).

2. Patrick F. Fagan et al., "The Real Root Causes of Violent Crime: The Breakdown of Marriage, Family, and Community," Heritage Foundation Backgrounder, March 1995, http://www.heritage.org/Research/Crime/BG1026.cfm (accessed September 17, 2007).

3. Ann Quigley, "Father's Absence Increases Daughter's Risk of Teen Pregnancy," Center for the Advancement of Health, and the Health Behavior News Service, May 14, 2003, http://www.cfah.org/hbns/news/daughter05-14-03.cfm (accessed September 10, 2007).

4. Mike McCormick and Glenn Sacks, "Why Dads Matter," *Houston Chronicle*, June 18, 2006, http://www.glennsacks.com/why_dads_matter.htm (accessed September 10, 2007).

5. Andrew J. Cherlin, *Marriage, Divorce, Remarriage*, revised and enlarged edition (Cambridge, MA: Harvard University Press, 1992). *See further:* "Although slave marriages and family ties lacked legal sanction, and owners were free to sell husbands away from wives and parents away from children, most African Americans married

and lived in two-parent households both before and after emancipation. Fathers played a larger familial role than previously thought. The nuclear family received support from an involved network of kin. Indeed, the kinship system forged under slavery would continue to function in twentieth-century rural and urban communities as a source of mutual assistance and cultural continuity." Mary Kupiec Cayton, Peter W. Williams, eds., "Family Structures," in *Encyclopedia of American Social History,* 3 vols. (Charles Scribner's Sons, Reproduced in the History Resource Center, Farmington Hills, MI: Gale Group) Archived at: http://galenet.galegroup.com/servlet/HistRC Document No. BT2313027032 (1993).

6. Fagan et al.

7. Joy Jones, "Marriage Is for White People," *Washington Post,* March 26, 2006; B1.

8. Ibid.

9. Fagan et al.

10. Andrew Hacker, *Mismatch: The Growing Gulf Between Women and Men* (New York: Scribner, 2003).

11. Jones, "Marriage Is for White People."

12. Juan Williams, *Enough: The Phony Leaders, Dead-End Movements, and Culture of Failure That Are Undermining Black America—and What We Can Do About It* (New York: Crown Publishers, 2006).

13. Michael Eric Dyson, *Is Bill Cosby Right? Or Has the Black Middle Class Lost Its Mind?* (New York: Basic Civitas Books, 2005).

14. Sarah H. Konrath, "Egos Inflating Over Time: Rising Narcissism and Its Implications for Self-Construal, Cognitive Style, and Behavior" (doctoral dissertation, University of Michigan, 2007), http://hdl.handle.net/2027.42/57606 (accessed February 18, 2008).

15. Muhammad Yunus with Alan Jolis, *Banker to the Poor: Micro-lending and the Battle Against World Poverty* (New York: Public Affairs Publishing, 1999). See also: Ishaan Tharoor, "Muhammad Yunus: A Nobel Laureate Banker Envisions an End to Poverty," *TIME,* Asia Edition. November 5, 2006, http://www.time.com/time/magazine/article/0,9171,1554973,00.html (accessed September 5, 2007).

[CHAPTER FOUR] A QUIET REVOLUTION

1. Hamburger and Wallsten, "GOP Sees a Future in Black Churches: Social Issues Are Binding the Party With a Group Once Firmly in the Democratic Camp."

2. Jackson, "New Black Church on Election Day."

3. Interview with Bishop Harry R. Jackson Jr., *The Tavis Smiley Show,* Black Entertainment Television (BET), February 3, 2005, http://www.pbs.org/kcet/tavissmiley/archive/200502/20050203_jackson.html (accessed March 4, 2008).

4. Tavis Smiley, *The Covenant With Black America* (Chicago: Third World Press, 2006). The elements of the covenant proposed by Tavis Smiley were more numerous and less specific than those we included in *The Black Contract with America on Moral Values.* Items included in Smiley's covenant included the following:

1. Securing the right to healthcare and well-being
2. Establishing a system of public education in which all children achieve at high levels and reach their full potential
3. Correcting the system of unequal justice
4. Fostering accountable, community-centered policing
5. Insuring broad access to affordable neighborhoods that connect to opportunity
6. Claiming our democracy
7. Strengthening our rural roots
8. Accessing good jobs, wealth, and economic prosperity

9. Assuring environmental justice for all

10. Closing the racial digital divide

5. Jill Lawrence, "Smiley: GOP Candidates Ignore Minorities," *USA Today*, September 13, 2007, http://www.usatoday.com/news/politics/election2008/2007 -09-13-tavis_N.htm?csp=34 (accessed September 13, 2007).

6. Edward Luce and Andrew Ward, "Republicans Shown Up by No-Show," *Financial Times*, September 29, 2007, http://www.ft.com/cms/s/0/7644c948-6e64- 11dc-b818-0000779fd2ac.html?nclick_check=1 (accessed March 8, 2008).

7. Michael Luo and Laurie Goodstein, "Emphasis Shift for New Breed of Evangelicals," *New York Times*, May 21, 2007. A1.

8. David Horowitz, "Hillary Clinton and 'The Third Way': How America's First Lady of the Left Has Bamboozled Liberals and Conservatives Alike," *FrontPage* magazine.com, June 22, 2000, http://www.frontpagemag.com/Articles/Read. aspx?GUID={BB3F7027-35CA-4777-8C3D-77B1494E4565} (accessed October 1, 2007).

9. George Barna, *The Frog in the Kettle* (Ventura, CA: Regal Books, 1990).

10. Thomas Sowell, "Hopelessly Devoted to Failure: The Left Today," *National Review*, August 21, 2007. http://article.nationalreview.com/?q= Mjc2NGM4NTBmYmUwYzRkYzNmMGVkMWZhYjU5ZjEzNDE= (accessed August 21, 2007).

11. Ibid.

12. Ibid.

13. Ibid.

14. In this regard, I would especially recommend the new book from Dr. James Bowman, a fellow of the Ethics and Public Policy Center in Washington and former American editor of the London Times *Literary Supplement*, which deals with the broad concept of honor and what it means to defend our God-given values in today's world. The book is: James Bowman, *Honor: A History* (New York: Encounter Books, 2006).

[CHAPTER FIVE] WHAT WE REALLY WANT

1. Jackie Calmes, "Bush's Conservative Base Frets: Key Issues Are Losing Focus," *Wall Street Journal*, January 25, 2007, http://online.wsj.com/public/article_print/ SB116969100575587100-xmhyV5Nts2GBEUw9o4X25gg0sWA_20070223.html (accessed October 22, 2007).

2. Tony Perkins, "Video Response to SOTU," Family Research Council, January 24, 2007, http://www.frcblog.com/2007/01/tony_perkins_video_response_to.html (accessed August 30, 2007).

3. Arthur C. Brooks, *Who Really Cares? The Surprising Truth About Compassionate Conservatism* (New York: Basic Books, 2006).

4. Frank Brieaddy, "Philanthropy Expert: Conservatives Are More Generous," Religion News Service, November 10, 2006, http://www.beliefnet.com/story/204/ story_20419_1.html (accessed Nov. 1, 2007).

5. Market Strategies, "Ohio Statewide Survey."

6. John Conyers Jr., *What Went Wrong in Ohio: The Conyers Report on the 2004 Presidential Election* (Chicago: Academy Chicago Publishers, 2005).

7. "President's Union Speech Pleases Conservative Base," *Washington Times*, January 26, 2007.

8. State of the Union 2007, http://www.whitehouse.gov/stateoftheunion/2007/ photoessay/06.html (accessed February 18, 2008).

9. Tony Perkins, "President's Speech Falls Short on Family," Family Research Council, January 23, 2007, http://www.frc.org/get.cfm?i=PR07A08&v=PRINT (accessed October 11, 2007).

10. J. David Kuo, *Tempting Faith: An Inside Story of Political Seduction* (New York: Free Press, 2006).

11. Lauren Dunn, "Five Minutes With David Kuo," *Campus-Progress*, January 3, 2007, http://campusprogress.org/features/1339/five-minutes-with-david-kuo (accessed September 11, 2007).

12. "Bribes + Vouchers = Black Bush Supporters," *The Black Commentator*, No. 124: February 3, 2005, http://www.blackcommentator.com/124/124_black_bush_supporters.html (accessed September 19, 2007). See also: Bill Berkowitz, "Cash & Carry: Bush, Blacks, and the Faith-Based Initiative," Media Transparency Web site, February 11, 2005, http://www.mediatransparency.org/pdastory.php?storyID=12 (accessed September 19, 2007).

13. Bill Sammon, "Bush Continues Outreach to Blacks," *Washington Times*, February 9, 2005.

14. Ibid.

[CHAPTER SIX] THE ELEPHANT IN THE ROOM

1. "What Is a Christian? New Moral Values; Evangelicals and Israel; End of Days; Capitalist Christian; The Seekers," *Anderson Cooper 360 Degrees*, CNN, December 14, 2006.

2. "What Would Jesus Really Do?" Roland Martin, host, CNN, April 8, 2007.

3. Lillian Kwon, "New Report Contradicts Past Claims of Black Church Decline," Christianpost.com, March 1, 2006, http://www.christianpost.com/pages/print .htm?aid=4059 (accessed September 21, 2007).

4. See, for example, Deuteronomy 6:24. When the Ten Commandments were handed down at Mt. Sinai, Moses instructed the people with these words: "And the Lord commanded us to observe all these statutes, to fear the Lord our God, *for our good always*, that He might preserve us alive, as it is this day" (emphasis added).

5. TeenMania.org, "Teen Mania's Mission Statement," http://www.teenmania .org/corporate/index.cfm (accessed February 8, 2008).

6. ChristianNewsToday,com, "See You at the Pole 2006: Be Still and Know," September 24, 2006, www.christiannewstoday.com/CWN1024.html (accessed February 18, 2008).

7. Audrey Barrick, "Study Reveals State of U.S. Church Planting," Christianpost .com, November 15, 2007, http://www.christianpost.com/article/20071115/30104_ Study_Reveals_State_of_U.S._Church_Planting.htm (accessed November 15, 2007).

8. Ibid.

9. Audrey Barrick, "Survey: Top Issues of Concern for American Evangelicals," Christianpost.com, October 1, 2007, http://www.christianpost.com/article/20071001 /29529_Survey%3A_Top_Issues_of_Concern_for_American_Evangelicals.htm (accessed November 15, 2007).

10. Jack Williams, "Study Finds Oceans Have Warmed," USAToday.com, August 11, 2005, http://www.usatoday.com/weather/climate/warmsea32300.htm (accessed February 18, 2008).

11. ChristianPost.com, "Evangelicals Least Concerned About Global Warming," September 19, 2007, www.christianpost.com/article/20070918/29346_Study:_ Evangelicals_Least_Concerned_about_Global_Warming.htm (accessed February 18, 2008).

12. Laurie Goodstein, "Evangelical Leaders Join Global Warming Initiative," *New York Times*, February 8, 2006, http://www.nytimes.com/2006/02/08/national/08warm

.html?ex=1297054800&en=c3998565b07f9657&ei=5088&partner=rssnyt&emc=rss (accessed October 8, 2007).

13. Greater Minnesota Association of Evangelicals, "Culture, Helping Hurting People, Evangelism, American Evangelicals Top Concerns," http://gmae .associationsonline.com/generic8.cfm (accessed February 18, 2008).

14. Scott Keeter et al., Social & Demographic Trends: "Blacks See Growing Values Gap Between Poor and Middle Class," Pew Research Center, November 13, 2007, http://pewresearch.org/pubs/634/black-public-opinion (accessed November 17, 2007).

15. Ibid.

16. Stephanie Simon and Mark Z. Barabak, "Evangelicals Flock on Their Own at the Polls," *Los Angeles Times*, November 15, 2007, http://www.latimes.com/news/ politics/la-na-evangelicals15nov15,0,4650045,full.story (accessed February 18, 2008).

[CHAPTER SEVEN] FREEDOM OF CONSCIENCE

1. BeyondMarriage.org, "Beyond Same-Sex Marriage," www.beyondmarriage .org/full_statement.html (accessed February 18, 2008).

2. Lou Chibbard Jr., "Gay Leaders Mobilize for Marriage Battle," *Washington Blade*, August 15, 2003, http://www.washblade.com/2003/8-15/news/national/ marrigefight.cfm (accessed August 28, 2007).

3. Ibid.

4. A comprehensive treatment of this and related issues can be found in Louis P. Sheldon, *The Agenda: The Homosexual Plan to Change America* (Lake Mary, FL: FrontLine Books, 2005), 61.

5. "Analysis and Conclusions of the Commission to Study All Aspects of Same Sex Civil Marriage and the Legal Equivalents Thereof, Whether Referred to as Civil Unions, Domestic Partnerships, or Otherwise" SB 427, Chapter 100:2, Laws of 2004. Commission Recommendation, Item 12, page 67.

6. Lou Chibbaro Jr., "Marriage Fight Heads to Legislatures in N.Y., Calif.," *Washington Blade*, July 14, 2006, http://www.afa.net/washingtonblade5pointplan .htm (accessed October 12, 2007).

7. Marshall Kirk and Erastes Pill, "The Overhauling of Straight America," *Guide* magazine, November 1987. Note also that Erastes Pill is a pseudonym of Harvard sociologist Hunter Madsen who coauthored the book, *After the Ball*, cited earlier.

8. Joe Kovacs, "God Invoked Constantly, 'Invisible' Candidates Who Failed to Show Still Get Tough Questions," LibertyPost.org, September 18, 2007, http://www .libertypost.org/cgi-bin/readart.cgi?ArtNum+200375 (accessed March 10, 2008).

9. Fred H. Cate, "The First Amendment and Compulsory Access to Cable Television," http://www.annenberg.northwestern.edu/pubs/cable/cable09.htm (accessed February 18, 2008).

10. Laurie Goodstein, "Senator Questioning Ministries on Spending," *New York Times*, November 7, 2007, http://www.nytimes.com/2007/11/07/us/07ministers.html ?ei=5088&en=0d5a53dc630f1afc&ex=1352091600&partner=rssnyt&emc=rss& pagewanted=print (accessed November 10, 2007).

11. United States Senate Committee on Finance, "Grassley Seeks Information From Six Media-based Ministries," November 6, 2007, http://www.senate.gov/ ~finance/press/Gpress/2007/prg110607.pdf (accessed February 12, 2008).

12. From Grassley's letter to Randy and Paula White. All letters to all six ministries contain similar verbiage, http://www.senate.gov/~finance/press/Gpress/2007/ prg110607a.pdf (accessed February 12, 2008).

[CHAPTER EIGHT] THE HEALTH-CARE CONUNDRUM

1. Laura Donnelly and Patrick Sawer, "Record Numbers Go Abroad for Health," *London Sunday Telegraph*, October 28, 2007 http://www.telegraph.co.uk/global/main .jhtml?xml=/global/2007/10/28/noindex/nhealth128.xml (accessed November 7, 2007).

2. "Presidential Candidates Health Care Proposals," National Association of Health Underwriters, September 2007, http://www.naschip.org/Chicago/presidential% 20Candidates%202008.pdf (accessed February 18, 2008).

3. Rudolph W. Guiliani, "A Free-Market Cure for US Healthcare System," *Boston Globe*, August 3, 2007, http://www.boston.com/news/nation/articles/2007/08/03/a_ free_market_cure_for_us_healthcare_system/ (accessed February 18, 2008).

4. "Issues: Health Care," Mike Huckabee for President, http://www .mikehuckabee.com/?FuseAction=Issues.View&Issue_id=8 (accessed February 18, 2008).

5. BlackHealthCare.com, "AIDS—Description: HIV Infection and AIDS," http:// www.blackhealthcare.com/BHC/AIDS/Description.asp (accessed February 18, 2008).

6. African American Health Center, NetWellness.org, http://www.netwellness .org/healthtopics/aahealth/ (accessed February 18, 2008).

7. Kaiser Communications on Key Facts: "Health Insurance Coverage and Access to Care Among African Americans," Henry J. Kaiser Family Foundation, June 2000, http://www.kff.org/uninsured/upload/Racial-and-Ethnic-Disparities-in-Access-to -Health-Insurance-and-Health-Care-Report.pdf (accessed November 10, 2007).

8. Centers for Disease Control, Office of Minority Health, Office of the Director, "Health Disparities Experienced by Black or African Americans—United States," http://www.cdc.gov/mmwr/preview/mmwrhtml/mm5401a1.htm (accessed February 18, 2008).

9. These and other data can be found at: http://www.kff.org/uninsured/1525 -index.cfm.

10. Douglas J. Besharov. "Beyond the Safety Net: A Brief Review Forty Years after the War on Poverty," American Enterprise Institute, July 12, 2007. The estimate of black poverty from this author's calculation is based on data from the U.S. Census Bureau, "Poverty 2005, Poverty Highlights, Detailed Tables," table POV01, August 29, 2006, available at http://www.census.gov/hhes/www/poverty/poverty05.html (accessed October 10, 2007).

11. "Health Insurance Coverage and Access to Care Among African Americans," drawn from E. R. Brown et al., "Racial and Ethnic Disparities in Access to Health Insurance and Health Care," UCLA Center for Health Policy Research and Kaiser Family Foundation, April 2000, http://www.kff.org/uninsured/upload/Health -Insurance-Coverage-and-Access-to-Care-Among-African-Americans.pdf (accessed March 4, 2008).

12. The White House, "President Bush Delivers State of the Union Address," http://www.whitehouse.gov/news/releases/2007/01/20070123-2.html (accessed February 18, 2008).

13. Ibid.

14. State Children's Health Insurance Program (SCHIP), National Conference of State Legislatures, http://www.ncsl.org/programs/health/chiphome.htm (accessed February 18, 2008).

15. White House Press Office, "President Bush Discusses SCHIP During Weekly Radio Address," October 6, 2007, http://www.whitehouse.gov/infocus/healthcare/ (accessed October 30, 2007).

16. See note 1, chapter 3.

17. The report, "Facts on Induced Abortion in the United States," from the Alan Guttmacher Institute shows that in 2008 African American women are 4.8 times more

likely than non-Hispanic whites to have an abortion; http://www.guttmacher.org/pubs/fb_induced_abortion.html (accessed March 4, 2008). See also: Health Statistics: "Abortion in the United States," Infoplease.com, http://www.infoplease.com/ipa/A0904509.html (accessed November 11, 2007).

18. Martin Luther King Jr., *A Testament of Hope: The Essential Writings and Speeches of Martin* (New York: HarperCollins, 1986), 300.

19. Colman McCarthy, "Jackson's Reversal on Abortion," *Washington Post*, May 21, 1988, http://swiss.csail.mit.edu/~rauch/nvp/consistent/mccarthy_jackson.html (accessed February 18, 2008).

20. For more information on the issue of "black genocide," visit the Life Education And Resource Network on the Internet (LEARN) at: http://blackgenocide.org/home.html.

21. Barna and Jackson, *High-Impact African-American Churches*.

22. David Crary, "Anti-Abortion Activists Eye Inner Cities," Associated Press, August 20, 2005, http://www.foxnews.com/printer_friendly_wires/2006Aug20/0,4675,AbortionInnerCities,00.html (accessed September 21, 2007).

23. Stephen Ohlemacher, "National Poverty Rate Declines," *Washington Post*, August 29, 2007, http://www.washingtonpost.com/wp-dyn/content/article/2007/08/28/AR2007082800610.html (accessed September 12, 2007).

24. Robert Rector, "Understanding Poverty and Economic Inequality in the United States," Heritage Foundation, November 5, 2004, http://www.heritage.org/Research/Welfare/bg1796.cfm (accessed November 12, 2007).

25. Walter Williams, "Are the Poor Getting Poorer?" *Human Events*, October 30, 2007, http://www.humanevents.com/article.php?id=23134 (accessed October 30, 2007).

[CHAPTER NINE] A TIPPING POINT FOR CONSERVATIVES

1. HUD.gov, "Secretary Jackson in Memphis," U.S. Department of Housing and Urban Development, August 7, 2007, http://www.hud.gov/news/speeches/2007-08-07.cfm (accessed November 11, 2007).

2. Ibid.

3. JBHE.com, "Doctoral Degree Awards to African Americans Reach Another All-Time High," *Journal of Blacks in Higher Education* (2006): http://www.jbhe.com/news_views/50_black_doctoraldegrees.html (accessed November 12, 2007).

4. Martin Luther King Jr, "I Have a Dream," August 28, 1963, http://www.americanrhetoric.com/speeches/mlkihaveadream.htm (accessed February 18, 2008).

5. Michael Jay Friedman, "The *Brown v. Board of Education* Decision—50 Years Later," U.S. Life, Culture and History, May 1, 2004, http://usinfo.state.gov/scv/history_geography_and_population/civil_rights/african_american_rights/brown_v_board_education.html (accessed February 18, 2008).

6. King, "I Have a Dream."

7. Stephen Thernstrom and Abigail Thernstrom, "The Consequences of Color-Blindness," *Wall Street Journal*, April 7, 1998, A18.

8. For an excellent discussion of the legal and ethical issues involved in such cases, see the book: J. Budziszewski, *Written on the Heart: The Case for Natural Law* (Downers Grove, IL: InterVarsity, 1997).

9. Malcolm Gladwell. *The Tipping Point: How Little Things Can Make a Big Difference* (Boston, MA: Little Brown, 2000).

10. Market Strategies, "Ohio Statewide Survey."

[CHAPTER TEN] THE WAY FORWARD

1. Harry R. Jackson Jr., "Jena Jigsaw," Townhall.com, September 24, 2007, http://www.townhall.com/columnists/HarryRJacksonJr/2007/09/24/jena_jigsaw (accessed March 4, 2008).

2. Craig Franklin, "Six Myths about the Jena 6: A Local Journalist Tells the Story You Haven't Heard," *Christian Science Monitor*, October 24, 2007, http://www.csmonitor.com/2007/1024/p09s01-coop.html (accessed October 30, 2007).

3. Manning Marable, "Race-ing Justice, Disenfranchising Lives: African Americans, Criminal Justice and the New Racial Domain," reproduced by *The Black Commentator* (from a lecture delivered at Fayetteville State University), November 14, 2006, http://www.blackcommentator.com/209/209_cover_race_ing_justice_marable_ed_bd.html (accessed November 6, 2007).

4. Human Rights Watch, "Race and Incarceration in the United States," February 26, 2002, http://www.hrw.org/backgrounder/usa/race/ (accessed March 4, 2008).

5. Ron Claassen, "Restorative Justice: Fundamental Principles." Center for Peacemaking and Conflict Studies, Fresno Pacific College. (A modified form of this list was presented at the U.N. Alliance of NGOs Working Party on Restorative Justice), May 1996.

6. Peter Biles, "Apartheid Crimes Dilemma Haunts SA," BBC News, Pretoria, August 11, 2007, http://news.bbc.co.uk/2/hi/programmes/from_our_own_correspondent/6940666.stm (accessed November 10, 2007).

HARRY R. JACKSON JR. IS SENIOR MINISTER OF HOPE CHRISTIAN Center in Beltsville, Maryland, and a bishop of the Fellowship of International Churches. He is a highly sought-after speaker on reconciliation and related topics and is a frequent contributor and guest of the major broadcast media. He is a columnist for Townhall .com, hosts a daily radio broadcast, and is the author of two previous books, including *The Black Contract With America on Moral Values* and *High-Impact African-American Churches*, with coauthor and researcher George Barna.

For more information on Bishop Jackson and the ministry of Hope Christian Center, please visit www.thehopeconnection.org.

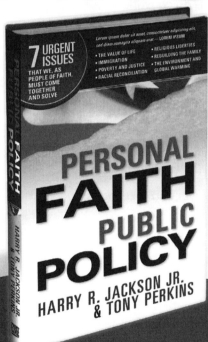